The Audience & the Playwright

The Audience & the Playwright

HOW TO GET THE MOST OUT OF LIVE THEATRE

MAYO SIMON

The Audience & The Playwright
How to get the most out of live theatre

Excerpts from *Oleanna* by David Mamet, copyright © 1992 by David Mamet. Used by permission of Pantheon Books, a division of Random House, Inc. Reprinted in the UK & Commonwealth (excluding Canada) by permission of Methuen Publishing Limited.

Excerpts from *Translations* by Brian Friel. Copyright © 1981 by Brian Friel. Reprinted by permission of Faber & Faber, Inc., an affiliate of Farrar, Straus and Giroux, LLC.

Library of Congress Cataloging-in-Publication Data:
Simon, Mayo.
The audience & the playwright : the theatrical experience observed /
by Mayo Simon.
    p. cm.
Includes index.
ISBN 1-55783-562-4
1. Theatre audiences. 2. Theatre audiences—Psychology. 3.
Drama—History and criticism. I. Title: Audience and the playwright.
II. Title.

PN2193.A8S57 2003
792'.01'9—dc21

                    2002153901

Applause Theatre & Cinema Books
151 West 46th Street, 8th Floor
New York, NY 10036
Phone: (212) 575-9265
Fax: (646) 562-5852
Email: info@applausepub.com
Internet: www.applausepub.com

Printed in Canada

SALES & DISTRIBUTION

North America:
HAL LEONARD CORP.
7777 West Bluemound Road
P. O. Box 13819
Milwaukee, WI 53213
Phone: (414) 774-3630
Fax: (414) 774-3259
Email: halinfo@halleonard.com
Internet: www.halleonard.com

UK:
ROUNDHOUSE PUBLISHING LTD.
Millstone, Limers Lane
Northam, North Devon Ex 39 2RG
Phone: (0) 1237-474-474
Fax: (0) 1237-474-774
Email: roundhouse.group@ukgateway.net

for Patty

Contents

Introduction

Why do you go to the theatre?

I know why I go. I write plays. Theatre is school for me. I have to see what's happening, if there's anything different, anything new I can—very discreetly—steal.

But what are you doing there?

People say, "I go to the theatre to relax, I go to forget my troubles, I go for entertainment. Besides, my spouse bought season tickets and this is our night."

Let's get serious. Was the last play you saw worth $150 for two tickets, plus the babysitter, the quick dinner, and the parking? And for what—for entertainment? To forget your troubles for an evening? And you can toss in getting exposed to important themes, serious ideas, experimental concepts, and literary values.

Is this why you go to the theatre?

I have an idea. Let's skip the theatre tonight. Let's spend a leisurely evening with friends. Remember the Tyrones in Connecticut? You haven't seen them in a long time. Let's drive up and have dinner.

James Tyrone is the famous actor with the lovely wife and the two sons. You'll get a kick out of the older one, Jamie. He's quite a wit. I'm not sure what he does. Edmund, the younger one, hasn't got much to say (he gets lots of colds), but they're always kidding each other and their father. Obviously, they have a great relationship. And Mary Tyrone, so gracious, so charming, reminds you a bit of Spring Byington with those fluttery hands, a dear really.

Their old summerhouse is wonderful, with a nice, warm, lived-in feeling. Perhaps a bit run down. The food's not too good either. You'll probably wonder for a moment if they're doing all right. Acting is a tricky business. But I hear that James does quite well in real estate.

A very pleasant evening, the old actor in good form, hearty, witty, full of stories. Good-natured bantering among the men as they share a whiskey (that boy should take some cough medicine), and affectionate teasing of the mother who can be a bit vague. Not like your family, with everyone at each other's throats. Afterwards, a long ride back to town, but no worse than the four-hour play you missed.

Now consider: What if you had gone somewhere else to see the Tyrones? Not at their home, but up on the stage in Eugene O'Neill's *Long Day's Journey into Night*. Very soon you'd discover that James Tyrone is an angry, tight-fisted, baffled man. His bitter son Jamie is an alcoholic with a wasted life. His tortured son Edmund has TB. And when his wife Mary comes down the stairs, her hands fluttering, you take one look and—Oh, God, something awful has happened to her. They can't bear to name it, but you're smart, you can guess what it is. She's on drugs again. You lean forward to watch this anguished, haunted, guilt-ridden family as they are forced to face the terrible truths about their lives. You watch with pity and compassion, and above all, with understanding.

Dinner in the country with O'Neill's fictional family, the Tyrones, brought little enlightenment. See them on the stage and a magical thing happens. Suddenly you have keen perceptions and penetrating insights. You can even congratulate yourself on your quickness and perspicacity.

How did you get so smart?

Well, occasionally you have sat in a room with others and noticed the little signals, the secret glances that let you understand that something was "going on." But in the ordinary course of life, how much do any of us notice?

I remember a graduate student who came to an end-of-semester party at my house. He stood by the fireplace with a drink in his hand complaining loudly about the idiots who ran the motion picture business and how stupid movies were and how there was never anything for intelligent people to see. After he was found dead, three months later, his diary revealed that on the night of the party he had been testing ropes to see which would be strong enough to not break when he threw himself out the window of his rooming house.

Some of us who had been there compared notes. What had he said? Were there any clues? Did anybody notice anything? No, nothing. That's how life is. But in the theatre...

In the theatre, you *see*. You see innocence and fragility, threats and hopes, illusions and reality. You see the terror and the suffering—and also the craziness and the comedy. When Trofimov, the student in act two of Chekhov's *The Cherry Orchard*, speaks passionately about his despair over a society where intelligent people philosophize endlessly and do nothing, you think, yes, yes, very true—and then you find yourself laughing as you note that Trofimov himself is relaxing in a garden, philosophizing endlessly and doing nothing.

How clever you feel. You laugh when no one on the stage is laughing. You cry when no one on the stage cries. Sometimes you feel an almost godlike understanding of people and events. The curious thing is, rarely does anyone on the stage see what you see and know what you know. When Oberon, the King of the Fairies in Shakespeare's *A Midsummer Night's Dream*, sees young lovers approaching, he stays to overhear their conversation, saying simply: "I am invisible"—invisible to every human on the stage, but quite visible to you. It's as though you—in your seat in the orchestra or balcony or boxes—have been placed in a privileged position, given extraordinary powers and asked to play a unique role.

Who put you in this privileged position? How did you get these powers? What is your role?

By the way, does this sound like sitting passively while you forget your troubles and enjoy the entertainment? Not at all. This sounds like being very alert, very engaged, very active. It even sounds like going to the theatre involves just a little bit of…work.

Why do you go to the theatre? You say it's entertainment and the hell with it. I say, there is pleasure and delight, of course. But where do pleasure and delight come from?

PART ONE

The Birth of the Audience

Seven-thirty: People are gathering on the sidewalk in front of the theatre. Clusters of strangers waiting for the doors to open. There are the three giggling girls from Queens at their first play. The elegant older couple who see everything. The middle-aged foursome studying the blow-up of the out-of-town reviews. The businessman who's had a rough day at the office and put down his credit card and does not want to think. Ten blue-haired ladies off the bus from Harrisburg. A handful of foreigners speaking an unidentified language. Two gay men in boots and earrings—one older, one younger—who know everyone in the company. Those who have been waiting months for this night, and those who just came from the half-price booth. Doctors with beepers. Hip high-school kids. People sleepy from too much dinner. Parents who brought a ten-year-old. Smart ones, dumb ones, excited ones, dull ones.

They don't know it, but in a few minutes they will walk into the theatre and, without a single rehearsal, assume a collective role that they will play perfectly. They will become an audience.

This is what's supposed to happen every night in the theatre. It actually happens on those occasions when the playwright constructs the proper relationship between the stage and the people in the seats. It's a mysterious and wonderful phenomenon. Audiences are made up of different people every night, and yet every night as the play unrolls their reactions are pretty much alike. Same laughter, same tears, same intense silences. When the play works, it works for everybody.

Yes, people are all different, but in many important ways we are the same. We all bring to the theatre the same human material: Memory. Anticipation. Hopes. Fears. Beliefs. And one powerful desire.

First, memory. You have some idea of the past. And even if you have a bad memory, you have a pretty good fix on the last fifteen minutes. Have you ever walked into a theatre fifteen minutes late? Got the time wrong. Couldn't find a parking space. Embarrassed, you slink down the aisle until you find your seat. Suddenly everybody is laughing. What's so funny? You concentrate on the stage looking for a clue. Obviously you've missed something. But what? What you've missed is the privileged information the playwright has prepared for you.

If you miss the phone calls at the start of Neil Simon's *The Odd Couple*, which establish that someone is suicidal, you won't know why the audience is laughing at the poker players shutting the windows when Felix Unger walks in. If you miss (or can't remember) the previous fifteen minutes or half-hour of any play, you're going to have problems in the theatre.

Second, anticipation. You remember the past; you anticipate the future. A man and a woman appear on the stage and begin to talk. You think— Oh, it's a love story. Or even—Oh, she's in danger. Anticipation creates suspense. Will the expected thing happen? And when it doesn't, that generates surprise. "Gee, I never thought it would turn out like that."

Only by expecting one thing can you be surprised by another. Basic rules: no anticipation, no surprise. No surprise, no delight.

Combine audience memory and anticipation with audience hopes and fears and you have the basic ingredients used by every playwright. In Edward Albee's *The Zoo Story*, a well-dressed man sits on a bench in the park as a scruffy man enters and starts talking. He paces around, asks odd questions, tells disturbing stories, and speaks of something mysterious that happened that day at the zoo. The two men are alone. You remember all those newspaper stories about the park. You anticipate violence. You want to shout down to the well-dressed innocent: "Stop talking and get out of there!"

You lean forward anxiously, a big step ahead of the innocent, and a big step behind the playwright. He'll tease your hopes and fears to create suspense (Will the innocent man be killed?), and then he'll surprise (and shock) you. Yes, someone is killed, but who would have thought...?

What works for tragedy works more intricately in comedy. Michael Frayn's *Noises Off* (1982, revised for Broadway 2001) is a play about a troupe of provincial actors struggling with a complicated English farce ("Nothing On"). During a rehearsal and two performances, lines get butchered, entrances are scrambled, props are mislaid or squashed or lost—while some of the actors sabotage the play and others try desperately to keep it going. As it gathers momentum and heads for disaster, *Noises Off* becomes a farce about a farce.

Question: How is the audience supposed to know all this? Neither you nor anyone else has ever seen "Nothing On", which is a parody of a fictitious English farce. When Tom Stoppard wrote *Rosencrantz and Guildenstern Are Dead*, he depended on the audience's memory of

Hamlet to make his comedic points. Here the playwright's first job is to create memory. He has to tell you enough about "Nothing On" so you'll know when things start going wrong. Describing this process will eliminate the humor, but it will give you an idea of how a comedy playwright instructs and entertains at the same time.

The curtain rises on the final rehearsal of "Nothing On." It's the night before the opening. While the actors are starting up the play, you get important information about them—who is deaf, who is dim-witted, who is in the middle of a lovers' quarrel, who is alcoholic, who faints at the sight of blood, who is blind without contact lenses, who hasn't learned the lines. These are called character set-ups. They will raise your fears, hopes, and expectations as you get your first look at the first act of "Nothing On."

Early in the play, Vicki, the bimbo of the farce, stares around the country house set she has just entered and remarks: "So many doors."

Doors are crucial in farce, which usually features people running in and out of them (in various states of undress). Vicki is being shown around by the real estate agent who has brought her here for some quick sex. As she learns the layout of the doors, so do you.

In the middle of the act, Vicki, now in her underwear, is pushed through the door to the linen cupboard by the real estate agent so the housekeeper (who has unexpectedly turned up carrying a plate of sardines) will not discover she's in the house. Then the wife of the owner of the house (who has turned up unexpectedly and doesn't know that anyone else is in the house, much less in the linen cupboard), accidentally locks Vicki in the cupboard. A few minutes later, Vicki knocks loudly at the cupboard door and is let out by the real estate agent who has forgotten he shoved her in there in the first place.

This is a farce set-up, one of many interlocking pieces of information that the playwright systematically inserts into your head, ready for instant recall as the play progresses. *Noises Off* is unusual because it features two kinds of set-ups—one for the farce that's being played, one for the actors who are playing it.

As you watch the six actors fumbling with doors and props—pick up the paper, leave the sardines—take the sardines, hang up the phone—come in through the window, go out through the study—you wonder how they can possibly keep everything in their heads. Add the explosive potential of their quirks and personal problems and you anticipate a disastrous first performance of "Nothing On."

Act two of *Noises Off* begins—surprise—several weeks later in the middle of the run. They have lived through the opening of "Nothing On"—but they are finding it impossible to live with each other. The stage set is now reversed—another surprise—so the real audience can see the madness that is developing backstage as the play is performed to an unseen audience. You have been "set-up." Now comes the "pay-off."

Furious bickering and jealous raging alternate between entrances almost missed and props remembered at the last moment. Close calls. Hairsbreadth escapes. You hope they can keep the show going, you fear some ghastly mistake. Who will have the first catastrophe? The drunk? The blind? The deaf? The dim-witted? It's like watching a careening car speeding on the wrong side of the highway. You know an accident is going to happen. You just don't know when.

Vicki gets shoved into the linen cupboard again. But this time she has to rush off to the dressing rooms to find someone who is asleep or drunk. She misses her cue to knock from inside the cupboard and she's not there when the door is opened, forcing the other actor to improvise awkwardly around her absence. Finally she appears backstage, gets into her underwear, and enters from the cupboard. You remember how the scene was supposed to go; you anticipate more desperate improvisation. Since Vicki is played by the dim-witted actress, you're ready for desperately dim-witted improvisation. Or, just possibly, she could come up with something clever that would get the play back on track. Instead she starts saying the exact lines she should have said five minutes before. In the face of disaster, she's pretending nothing has happened. That's a surprise nobody anticipated, and it produces a totally unnerved "...What?" from the other actor and huge laughter in the audience. (Since the farce she's playing in is also about people carrying on normally in the midst of chaos, it's a doubly witty moment.)

In act three, the handle comes off the cupboard door and Vicki is *really* trapped inside and—Well, you get the idea. One laugh sets up the next anticipation that sets up hopes and fears that set up the next surprise that sets up the next laugh. Multiply set-ups and payoffs by fifty and you get a notion of the complexity of *Noises Off,* which you—the audience—will follow perfectly without rehearsal. Such is the power of your privileged seat in the theatre.

I've been describing playwright tactics. They work for Michael Frayn, they work for Albee, they work for Neil Simon, and they work for Shakespeare and Sophocles. All playwrights—ancient, modern, serious, and trivial—use memory, anticipation, and hopes and fears to help the audience play its part.

Memory is built into us. Anticipation we learn. Hopes and fears spring from our common beliefs about life. Most of us believe that life is precious. Most of us believe life is temporary. We only go around once. Dead is dead. Without these beliefs, there's not much in the way of drama. How tragic is Hamlet's death if he gets another chance in another life?

It may be that all civilization, all our urges to perpetuate ourselves, all culture, religion, society, art, science, technology, wars, everything (including theatre), can be traced to the irreconcilable tension between the consciousness of self and the knowledge that the self doesn't last. But most playwrights aren't deep thinkers. They're foot soldiers in the trenches, picking up useful knowledge and running with it. Not so much interested in the theory of warfare as in trying to stay alive.

Other common beliefs that playwrights use: We believe there are natural ties that bind, especially in families. We believe in the power of commitments formed by marriage and romantic love. A visitor from another planet where there are no families, no marriages, no love, would find many of our dramas tough to understand. Oedipus discovers he's killed his father and married his mother, so he tears out his eyes. What's the big deal? Othello thinks his wife is unfaithful, so he strangles her. Strange. Romeo kills himself when he thinks Juliet is dead. Why? Medea kills her children when her husband leaves her for another woman. Yawn.

There were once strong ties between teacher and student, master and apprentice. Not too much in the Mr. Chips line anymore. Ties between man and God were vital to Greek drama and the miracle and mystery plays of the thirteenth century. Outside of an occasional Amadeus, that sort of play is rare now.

Friendship still matters. Clan and ethnic ties are important to some, patriotism to others. But the measuring stick of all human bonds is the binding power of family. When family ties are tested or violated, drama begins. Think *Hamlet, Oedipus the King, Othello, Medea, Long Day's Journey into Night, The Odd Couple, The Cherry Orchard, King Lear, Macbeth, The Tempest, A Doll's House, Hedda Gabler, The Three Sisters, The Seagull, Uncle Vanya, The Father, Desire Under the Elms, Lost in Yonkers, 'Night, Mother, Betrayal, Same Time...Next Year,* etc., etc., etc.

More beliefs we bring to the theatre: We believe in happiness, though we're aware of tragedy. We believe in success, though we know it comes at a price. We believe in consequences, though we love a good fight. We believe that one life can deeply affect another. We believe in a rough kind of justice. We believe ourselves to be realistic, commonsensical, shrewd assessors of others. We believe that certain urges motivate people to action: sex, money, power, revenge. Sometimes an urge to do evil. Occasionally an urge to do good.

These common beliefs are the foundation of most plays. But no play will live and breathe without the fuel supplied by the audience's one basic unstated yet powerful desire. What do you want when you go to the theatre? To be amused? To forget your problems? I don't think so. The desire of the audience is to understand.

The strength of the audience's desire to understand can be measured by the playwright's use of the tactic of withholding. The playwright tantalizes, teases, even frustrates in order to raise the stakes, to make you care more and more about reaching that final moment of illumination.

Samuel Beckett is the modern master of withholding. The two tramps in *Waiting for Godot* wait...and wait...and wait...and wait for the mysterious Mr. Godot to arrive, and you wait wait wait wait with them—touched, amused, frustrated, and finally desperate for someone to come and explain the point of it all. Over and over again the motif is repeated:

> ESTRAGON: I'm tired! *(Pause)* Let's go.
> VLADIMIR: We can't.
> ESTRAGON: Why not?
> VLADIMIR: We're waiting for Godot.
> ESTRAGON: Ah! *(Pause. Despairing.)* What'll we do, what'll we do!
> VLADIMIR: There's nothing we can do.
> ESTRAGON: But I can't go on like this.
> VLADIMIR: Would you like a radish?

The wrong person arrives. Or is it the right person? Or is there a right person? By the end you realize you have absorbed Beckett's bleak, sad, funny, bracing vision of what life is about.

In the ordinary world you rarely get any kind of vision. Life is too confused, too messy, too many unknowns, too much background noise. It's in the theatre that you get a chance to see clearly. Theatre clarifies life.

Still want to talk about entertainment? Fine. Just realize what entertainment is based on: Understanding. You don't laugh at the joke until you "get it."

It is out of your desire to understand that the playwright constructs your role. It's not easy. If he gives you too much to do, you'll get annoyed, too little and you'll start inventing your own role, which usually means laughing at the wrong lines, or thinking about business or sex or dinner. But when the playwright gets it just right, you play your part eagerly and with great pleasure.

No doubt there are differences between today's audience and audiences of a hundred years ago, or a thousand years ago, or twenty-five hundred years ago. Nevertheless, all playwrights everywhere have had to deal with the same problem—how to keep them in their seats—which they have all solved the same way, by giving the audience a powerful role.

As for the play tonight, it's a new work in preview, and I hear your part is outstanding.

Seven-forty: The house is open. You can go in now.

Stages

There's something special about a theatre: plain or fancy; benches for fifty or tailored seats for a thousand; Shakespearean thrust or Greek amphitheatre or in-the-round or basement platform or picture frame with an elegant proscenium and terra-cotta angels blowing trumpets. Whether it's steel and glass, or plaster and plush, lit by candles or lit by lasers, theatres haven't changed very much in twenty-five hundred years. Live performers up there, live audience down here.

I've heard it said that the theatre is out of date, and that eventually all drama will be brought to us on screens, little screens at home or big screens in the movie house. Trust me, it won't be the same. What works on a stage doesn't work (or doesn't work the same way) anywhere else.

I remember seeing *Death of a Salesman* on television. Along with several million others (probably more people than ever saw it in the theatre), I watched Arthur Miller's great play in my living room. The actors were coming off a successful Broadway revival. Not a line in the play had been changed. But something was clearly wrong. The surreal settings (redesigned for television), combining reality and fantasy, came across as artificial and puny. The dialogue, which had moved me to tears the first time I heard it in a theatre, now seemed—well—theatrical. Blown up.

Unreal. The big climaxes were overwrought—closer to a parody of a play than a play. Miller's words, his plot, his characters, the rise and fall of his scenes, just didn't fit well on the little screen. The added camera movements, movie-style cuts, close-ups, and dissolves only emphasized the awkwardness of this intruder from another world.

Many years ago, NBC, in a high-minded move, produced a whole season of televised plays. None of them were very successful. I remember one, *All the Way Home*, Tad Mosel's sensitive adaptation of James Agee's *A Death in the Family*, in which the stage sets had broken walls and no ceilings, and four chairs stood in for a car. What was fine in a theatre became off-putting, even silly, in my living room.

And that's the point: Sitting at home surrounded by the normal clutter of sights and sounds—the dishwasher in the kitchen, the heat coming from the vents, the cars in the street—it's natural to judge what we see on television by the life around us. If the one is not something like the other, then it's not real. "Not real" is maybe the wrong phrase. "Not believable" is more accurate. We want to believe what we see. When we see an Ionesco play on the stage, we know it's not real, but we're in his universe and we accept it. In the same way we accept an empty stage for a battlefield and a hand held to the ear for a telephone. Seen on a screen in your living room, a stage set in which four chairs are supposed to be an automobile only serves to make your spouse grumble, "What's the matter, they couldn't afford a car?"

Television can transport us across vast distances. *Masterpiece Theater* takes us to the past, *Star Trek* to the future. These shows can expand our view of the possibilities of life. The sets are solid—there are walls, ceilings, objects, vistas. As in the rest of television, everything is quite concrete. We demand concreteness from the little screen. Anything else feels awkward. (Even televised fantasies like the Mary Martin *Peter Pan* usually begin with a solid reality setting.)

Maybe we should try a bigger screen.

I think it's always a good idea to make some sort of commitment before experiencing art. It takes us out of the ordinary, prepares us for something new. So let's drive to the mall, buy tickets at the Cineplex (moderate but meaningful commitments), and look for which one of the twenty-five viewing rooms is showing our movie.

When I was a kid in Chicago, motion picture theatres were great ornate temples. Goldfish and swans in the lobby, paintings by real artists in the corridors, rose and gold carpets, thickets of chandeliers, plush seats. What's fancy now at the Cineplex is the food. But let's skip the cappuccino and the giant cookies and the calamari. Maybe a box of popcorn and a Coke, then we'll go in.

Did you ever notice where you sit in a movie house? I don't mean back or front, I mean in relation to others. Most people will sit apart, by themselves or with a friend. It's just you and the screen. In the theatre you don't mind sitting next to a stranger. Theatre is a group experience. When the group sees something enjoyable, it lets the stage know and the stage responds. You can feel the charges of electricity jolting back and forth between stage and audience. Very little applause in the movie house. Nobody up there to respond. It's a one-way experience for one.

You have fifteen minutes before the movie begins to eat your popcorn and watch ads for eye surgeons, trivia quizzes, and pleas to be quiet ("Remember, you're not at home"). Then previews of coming attractions—the same ones you saw last week and the week before that and the week before that. Finally—loud music and loud loud graphics—the FEATURE PRESENTATION!

Thank God, the movie.

Is it different than television? It should be, at ten dollars a ticket. In today's hi-tech world, with huge screens and surround sound, the audience can experience everything: earthquakes, explosions, burning cities, tidal waves, the insides of tornadoes, wars with fantastic weapons, giant reptiles/fish/worms, heads splitting, arms ripped off, blood spurting; and of course everything intimate, every bodily function, including sex—especially sex—every kind of sex. Nothing held back. Casts of thousands. Costs in the millions. And it's all up there on the screen.

Is it satisfying? Millions of people think so. But for many others there's still something missing at the movies.

Take your seat in the theatre. Look around. It's cut off from the ordinary world, quiet, softly lit. No eating, no drinking, no ads on a screen.

Down there in front of you is a blank space, the stage. Sometimes it's bare and empty, or with the set revealed in a provocative light. Sometimes a curtain conceals everything. There's a soft buzz as the audience gathers and settles down. There's a sense of expectation. You've made a sizable commitment, four or five or six times what you pay for a movie. Will it be worth it? Is there something so special about being in a theatre? What does the stage offer that can't be done a thousand times better on a screen?

Let's do some comparison-shopping. Let's take one aspect of a story that began as a stage play, then was video taped for television, and finally became a film, and note how the audience is affected in each case.

The Elephant Man by Bernard Pomerance (Tony Award 1979, revived on Broadway 2002) opened at the Hampstead Theatre in London. Philip Anglim, an American actor, optioned it for himself and produced it in the basement of a church in New York City. The critics came, were dazzled, and it reopened on Broadway in April 1979.

The Elephant Man is about John Merrick, the world's most deformed man, thought to be an imbecile, and Frederick Treves, a nineteenth-century London doctor who protects him from a hostile world, discovers his intelligence and sensitivity, and sees him turn (for a short time) into a Victorian celebrity. Most of the play takes place in a minimalist abstraction of a hospital. A cello is heard between the scenes to keep your heart in the right place.

Treves introduces the elephant man with a clinical lecture using photographic slides to demonstrate his deformities in hideous detail. And yet, when you get your first sight of him, backstage in a freak show, you see something quite different from that which you were prepared for. He is twisted up physically, but when you look at his face you see—surprise—a young man who is not at all deformed. In fact the elephant man is quite good-looking.

Strange, isn't it? People, even other doctors, look away in horror or turn on him in rage. But from your privileged position, you realize—and this is really extraordinary because no one says it and it's not in the script—you realize that they are seeing his outer form, while you are seeing his inner self, his spirit, and that is beautiful. (The script does give a hint: Treves mentions his one perfect arm and hand, as though the beautiful inner man is trying to break through the shell of his ugly body.)

Who told you all this? Nobody told you. You just understand, and they don't. How delicious. Those dummies on the stage—smart ones, stupid ones—they don't get it. You ordinary people, you the audience—and all of you together—you get it. How smart you are in the theatre. How satisfying to be in such a privileged position.

Cut to the television screen. The exact same sequence taken right off the stage. The characters on the screen look at the elephant man and see hideous, while you see...Well, what do you see? Your spouse who comes into the TV room from washing the car says, "That's the ugliest man in the world? Doesn't look that bad to me. Maybe it's a bad make-up job."

You're not sure what you're supposed to think. You've lost the understanding that you are seeing the elephant man's inner life, his spirit, while the others see only his outward ugliness. What's the problem? What happened to your privileged position? Can it be that something in you is being defeated by your surroundings, by the sights and sounds you live with?

Cut to the big movie screen. David Lynch's 1980 film-version of *The Elephant Man* has the same story, same characters, different dialogue, different build up, and a truly ugly elephant man. Turning to your spouse, you say: "That's really ugly. Reminds me of your Aunt Bessie." "Shhh!" says someone behind you. Somebody else starts to giggle.

What's going on here?

The screen is very specific. A handsome man portrayed as ugly or an ugly man presented as handsome would just be confusing. The screen says this one is ugly, and by golly the screen is right. And how do you respond to ugly? Some will feel pity. Some will be embarrassed. Where's your privileged position? You have none. You see what the characters see. You tag along emotionally with Treves, the sympathetic doctor, as he discovers the intelligence and sensitivity trapped inside the elephant man.

This is a beautifully made film, but the unique position you had in the play is gone. To make up for this, outside threats will be added that only you are aware of—bad guys who want to exploit him again as a freak— a weak substitute for your powerful place in the play.

Back to the stage: A nurse enters to look after the elephant man. She's been warned about his hideous deformities. Don't worry, she says, she's lived in Africa with the most horrible forms of leprosy. Nothing bothers her. She approaches the elephant man with a tray of food. He turns to face her. Up in the air goes the tray and the terrified nurse runs from the room screaming. She doesn't see how beautiful he is. You laugh at the nurse, and feel very good about yourself. Finally, an actress enters who sees what you see and is at ease with the elephant man. You smile and admit her to the club of sensitive, insightful people.

(Bonus thought: After you leave the theatre, you might pause for a moment at the next horrible looking bum who puts his hand out for money, and for just a moment you might look at him and wonder...Nah, that only works in the theatre.)

What is the theatre doing that TV and film are not? The theatre is liberating your imagination. No matter who you are or what your state of mind, as soon as you take your seat in the theatre, something extraordinary happens:

> O for a muse of fire, that would ascend
> The brightest heaven of invention:
> A kingdom for a stage, princes to act,
> And monarchs to behold the swelling scene.
> Then should the warlike Harry, like himself,
> Assume the port of Mars, and at his heels,
> Leashed in like hounds, should famine, sword, and fire

Crouch for employment. But pardon, gentles all,
The flat unraised spirits that hath dared
On this unworthy scaffold to bring forth
So great an object. Can this cock-pit hold
The vasty fields of France? Or may we cram
Within this wooden O the very casques
That did affright the air at Agincourt?

The answer to Shakespeare's Chorus in *Henry the Fifth* is, "Yes! Yes! Yes!"

How does it work? How does taking your seat in a theatre liberate your imagination? I have no idea. But without it, the playwright can't do his job and you can't do yours. Maybe it has to do with being on neutral ground, away from the real world. Maybe it's just a theatrical convention, an unspoken agreement that the audience makes with the stage. Whatever it is, it's the most potent thing the playwright has going for him. As Shakespeare demonstrates over and over, the playwright uses the audience's imagination to make giant leaps from the seen to the unseen, and what is more important, giant leaps to the insights you'll need to play your part.

How many of Shakespeare's plays have been put on the screen in an attempt to capture on film those qualities that enchant audiences in the theatre, and with what results? I've just seen the latest: *A Midsummer Night's Dream*, with an all-star cast, set in lush Italian countryside. And it still doesn't work.

The movie, with its real villa, real statues, real vistas under a real sky, makes us apply realistic standards of behavior to a non-natural stage presentation. In the first scene, in an ornate room filled with heavy furniture, an angry father leaves a daughter alone with her lover, allowing them to plot their escape. We don't believe it for a second. Same scene in the play, no problem. The minimal stage world creates its own logic. The demands of the real world are relaxed and put to sleep. Imagination flourishes.

The film presents the fairyland in the woods with great beauty, gorgeous costumes, opulent settings. It's not close to the effect produced by Shakespeare's words and your imagination. In the play, the mismatched enchanted lovers are romantic and hilarious. In the film, the same characters wandering in realistic woods on bicycles (don't ask) struggle awkwardly to make their scenes work. The natural world is passing critical judgment on action created for the stage. Imagination is stifled.

On the other hand, Laurence Olivier starts his film of *Henry the Fifth* on an Elizabethan stage and then dissolves into the three dimensional world with the invasion of France, to show that film can do what the stage can not. But it's all on film of course, and looking at a filmed stage, as we've noted, does not liberate the imagination.

The motion picture, with its shifting frames of reference, can take us anywhere and show us anything, and that is its glory. What seems to be the limitation of the theatre can—by using the power of your imagination—become its greatest asset.

It can bring instant understanding, as in *The Elephant Man*, where you, the privileged audience, see something inside a man that others on the stage do not. It can move you from the tiniest visual or auditory clue to revealing insights about people and relationships. It can fill in the details of a setting that presents only the barest outline on the stage. It can make you accept day for night, a few for many, men for women, young for old.

"Well, this is the forest of Arden," says Rosalind in *As You Like It*, and the scene is magically set. Of course, this only works in a wood-and-straw Elizabethan theatre or an open modern stage. Then the line is witty and does wonders for your imagination. Let Rosalind look around at a real forest (Have you ever seen a movie version?) and Shakespeare's line becomes a redundant brick.

In *Cloud Nine*, Caryl Churchill's fantastical play, women play men, men play children, a doll becomes a living character, people meet themselves at different ages. The imagination leaps in understanding, and the audience follows easily what would be silly or confusing on film.

Edmund Tyrone, the younger son in O'Neill's *Long Day's Journey into Night*, is heard coughing off-stage before he enters. Every sound in the theatre is meaningful; nobody has to explain that cough to you. When Edmund finally coughs on stage the effect is piercing. (In the film version, he is also heard and seen coughing, but the effect is mild compared with the heart-wrenching off-stage sound in the theatre. Go figure.)

All playwrights use your imagination to connect offstage with onstage. Mel Edison, the anxious, depressed, out-of-work executive trapped in his Manhattan apartment in Neil Simon's *The Prisoner of Second Avenue*, is assaulted on every side by the unseen madness of urban life: unbearable heat, malfunctioning appliances, decaying garbage, and crazy neighbors pouring water on his terrace and pounding on his paper-thin walls. A man's life is unraveling in a giant dysfunctional city, and it's all created in your imagination. As so often happens in Neil Simon's work, the effect is both disturbing and hilarious.

Neil Simon is an expert at using the proscenium frame to create comedy out of what you don't see. Take a simple thing like an entrance. A door opens, someone appears. From where? What's out there? You can't see it but what you imagine often produces a laugh, especially when you anticipate one thing and something else happens.

Example: The stage set for *Barefoot in the Park* is an apartment on the top floor of a New York walk-up. The humor comes from imagining people climbing five flights of stairs. Each entrance is a witty variation on exhaustion.

Nobody is seen climbing. You only see people entering. You begin to anticipate what people are going to look like when they appear. Each time the buzzer rings and voices from the ground floor are heard, you laugh. They're so innocent down there, they don't know what they're in for. But you're smart, you know. Then, just when you anticipate one more hilarious variation on exhaustion, the playwright surprises you with someone who walks in showing no effects at all and you laugh with delight at yourselves. So smart, but not as smart as Neil Simon.

Actually watching people climb stairs becomes tedious very quickly, as you will discover if you rent the movie and look at it, and then remember how funny each entrance was on the stage.

Consider exits: Someone leaves the stage. To where? Trofimov, the student in Chekhov's *The Cherry Orchard* stomps off in a fury in act three. He's getting out of that house! When you hear him falling down the stairs, you laugh. It's amusing to imagine the klutzy, self-important student trying to make a strong exit and ending up looking foolish. I don't think you'd want to actually see it. It would be painful, not funny, probably sad.

There are two other key areas that the stage almost always leaves to the imagination. Sex, because it can get embarrassing if you're too close to it, which could lead to laughter at the wrong moments; violence because it's messy and doesn't always work right on the stage and therefore it's not always believable. You never see Oedipus gouging his eyes out. Would you like to, on the stage, right in front of you? I don't think so.

The Elizabethans liked gore. John Webster made a career out of bloody murders and torture. Even Shakespeare enjoyed it occasionally. In the text of *King Lear* (act three, scene seven), the Earl of Gloucester's eyes are pulled out one at a time and stamped on. Ugh! But when I've watched it in a modern production, the actors have had their backs turned and all that's exposed is the horrific result.

I know that in the age of experimental theatre there are stages somewhere filled with simulated or real blood. But generally speaking, today's audience prefers to use its imagination. Watching Martin McDonagh's play, *The Beauty Queen of Leenane* (1996), you anticipate the bloody murder of a mother by her daughter. The mother appears to be sleeping in a rocking chair. The daughter talks quietly, holding a fireplace poker. You start backing away from what you don't want to see. The daughter raises the poker over her head...and the mother keels over. The murder has already taken place. The scene is grisly, but watchable, and controllable and believable. The playwright has surprised you. Your imagination bridges the gap between intention and execution.

This is doubly true when it comes to sex on the stage. In all of Shakespeare's celebrated love dramas, there are no sex scenes. Who would actually like to watch middle-aged paunchy Antony doing it with forty-something Cleopatra? Even young and beautiful Romeo and Juliet have only one brief bed scene, just after sex. (Yes, female characters were played by men, but that doesn't change the point.) Occasionally in the modern theatre there are scenes that get pretty close to the real thing. In this department the movies have it all over the stage. What would make you turn away with embarrassment if you saw it in the theatre makes you lean forward with interest (probably prurient, but what the hell) when you see it on the screen. Much more about this later.

When the theatre does not trust the audience's imagination, the results are usually not very good. In the 1996 Broadway revival of Noël Coward's *Present Laughter*, sex was put right on the stage, almost in your face. Here is Garry Essendine, suave man of the theatre, humping a woman on a couch, zipper down, skirt up. Unfortunate and embarrassing, even with their backs to us.

On the London stage in the 1940s, Garry Essendine, wearing a smoking jacket, actually touched a fully dressed woman's thigh (while talking about something else of course) producing a huge charge of sexuality that made the audience take in its collective breath. In the theatre, the imagined is more powerful than the observed.

Fifty years ago motion pictures were more theatrical, that is to say, they left something to the imagination. George Stevens' 1953 classic western *Shane* gave us a whole love story in which the only physical contacts between Alan Ladd and Jean Arthur are a country dance and a handshake. Everything else is in the audience's mind. In those days, the camera too was more reticent. Remember the Humphrey Bogart–Mary Aster embrace in John Huston's 1941 film *The Maltese Falcon*? As his head lowers toward her lips, the camera moves slowly forward concealing the lovers on the couch while it stares through the blowing window curtain at the gunman below, standing in a doorway under a street lamp, looking up at them. Pretty sexy stuff.

Do you remember the famous first kiss between Cary Grant and Deborah Kerr in Leo McCarey's 1957 romance *An Affair to Remember*? If you do, think again—because it's not on the screen. After teasing the audience with a half-hour of shipboard flirtation and passionate eye contact, the moment finally arrives as Cary Grant is following Deborah Kerr up the ship's ladder from one deck to another. The camera does not move with them. It appears that they will continue up and out of the scene—and then they stop. All you see is their legs.

How do you know they're kissing? Cary Grant's one foot is dangling in the air and his other foot is pressed against a rung of the ladder, and you feel (but do not see) him reaching up to her face. A famous romantic moment that's all in your imagination.

But who could forget Barbara Stanwyck's glittering eyes staring straight ahead in Billy Wilder's 1944 film noir *Double Indemnity*, as you hear but do not see her lover strangling her husband. Or the death scene on the Warsaw theatre stage in Ernst Lubitsch's 1942 film of Nazi occupiers and Polish actors, *To Be or Not to Be*. Lubitsch was the master of using the camera to set loose audience imagination. Here, at the climax of a chase scene in a theatre, pistol shots and a scream of pain are heard. You're desperate to find out who's been hurt in the unseen backstage shootout between the Polish patriot and the Gestapo officer. Someone shouts: "Raise the curtain!" The camera frames the stage curtain as it rises to reveal the two men standing motionless like actors in a scene. The Gestapo officer collapses and dies. The mess of struggle and violence is off-screen, just as it would be in a play. You see the grim after-effects framed by the calm camera eye. That the scene takes place on a stage makes the action both shockingly theatrical and also quite witty. The Lubitsch touch.

That's all over now. They don't make 1940s black and white films anymore. Mike Nichols, in his 1971 film *Carnal Knowledge*, uses the close-up camera eye several times to create a restricted point of view, like the screen version of a stage frame, as one character reacts to other characters who are unseen, forcing your imagination to go to work.

Candice Bergen laughs hysterically at the off-screen actions of her two lovers. Jack Nicholson stares straight ahead as Candice Bergen and Art Garfunkel are heard packing for a trip that will confirm the end of his affair with her. Two women watch an unseen tennis game between Nicholson and Garfunkel, one sizing them up with interest, one turning away in pain. This combination of film and stage technique works well for a while. After the third or fourth scene it begins calling attention to itself as technique rather than story telling.

The audience in the movie house wants to see it all. But there are still occasions when a film makes effective use of something the audience does not actually observe. The most exciting moment in *Star Wars* was not a super-elaborate feast-for-the-eyes special effect. It was the move to hyper-speed, which was accomplished with a simple visual, a sound effect, and a maximum of viewer imagination.

In the 1950s, plays began trying to imitate films using multiple sets on turntables and levels. That only emphasized what the stage was not—a window on everything. Now the stage has learned something much more important from film—how to create fluid changes of time and space without distinct entrances and exits, and this has given rise to whole new techniques for storytelling. With thrust stages and theatres in the round, the actual frame has disappeared. Nevertheless the essential character of the theatre remains the same. It's a place where imagination flourishes. Only in the theatre can the audience in its privileged position see literally into someone's soul. Only in the theatre—

Hold on. The lights are starting to dim. It's five after eight. Latecomers are scrambling into their seats. A quick look at the program: the place, the time, the director, the cast. Your name isn't listed, but your role starts when the curtain goes up.

The theatre is in black.

Silence.

Something's going to happen.

PART TWO

Beginnings

In the first scene of Ibsen's *Hedda Gabler*, after Hedda is introduced with irritation for her new maid, sarcasm for her new husband, and well-bred condescension for an old lady's new hat, she finds herself alone in the drawing room of her new house. Suddenly she raises her hands in a gesture of despair and stares out the windows like a trapped animal. Who sees this? Only the audience. You—and only you—are aware that under Hedda's fastidious distaste for middle class life, something desperate is going on.

Beginnings are wonderful. The lights pop up, and instantly you're in the middle of other people's lives. Every word, every gesture, is designed to give you the special knowledge that puts you in your privileged place and starts you in your role. And what precisely is that role at the beginning of a play? Let's look at some more openings.

Eugene O'Neill's *Long Day's Journey into Night* also begins with a wordless clue. Mary Tyrone and her husband James appear from their unseen dining room chattering about the breakfast they've just finished. But your eye goes instantly to her nervous hands as they flit and flutter out of control. Strangely, James seems not to notice what you can't avoid seeing. This makes the conversation bogus, even ominous. Something is happening that he can't face. What is it? And how long can he avoid it?

Another opening gesture: In the first scene of Arthur Miller's *Death of a Salesman*, Willie Loman appears carrying two heavy sample cases which he sets down with an audible expression of exhaustion. Who sees this? Only you. He's at the end of his rope. He's also filled with crazed dreams of success. The split between his illusions and reality is becoming unbearable. What's he going to do?

Marsha Norman's *'Night, Mother* (Pulitzer Prize 1983) opens on Thelma Cates unwrapping a cupcake and her daughter Jessie, who has cerebral palsy, looking for and then finding a gun. Thelma, concerned about her manicure, casually asks what the gun's for. Jessie says: "The gun is for me." The mother doesn't get it. You do. The daughter is planning to kill herself. You want to know why, and can she be stopped?

Garson Kanin's 1946 classic political comedy *Born Yesterday* begins with a conversation between a reporter and a maid in an elaborate Washington hotel suite. They're talking about a junk dealer named Harry Brock, a World War Two millionaire (ill-gotten gains?) who is paying an obscene amount of money to live in this hotel (What's he up to?). By the time Harry enters, talking like a saloon bouncer, snapping his fingers at his lackeys, and pretending that he's not impressed with the suite, you recognize him as a crude bully. You wonder if he'll be making a dirty deal in your Capital City. And who is that cute blond who came in with him?

Sophocles' *Oedipus the King* begins with a long dialogue between the world's wisest and greatest king and a chorus of despondent priests. There is plague in the city. Everyone is dying. The priests have come to beg Oedipus to save his people as he has done in the past. Oedipus tells them he's appealed to the god at Delphi and will do all the god commands.

Then his brother-in-law Creon appears with the god's words. The plague has come because an ancient murder has gone unavenged. The murderer must be banished or killed. But who is the murderer? And how is he to be found after so many years?

Stop for a moment. You're fifteen minutes into the play—do you know more than anyone on the stage? Has someone important been put into context for you? Have you been placed in a privileged seat? Apparently not. And yet, if you were in the audience 2,400 years ago when *Oedipus the King* opened at the festival of Dionysus in Athens, you would have known the story of Oedipus. Every Greek knew the Oedipus myth. When the chorus spoke of his greatness and called him "the first of men," the Athenian audience knew that by the end of the play Oedipus would be scorned as the lowest of men. And when Oedipus put a curse on the unknown murderer, they knew the curse would fall on Oedipus himself. Oedipus was smart; the audience was smarter.

It still didn't know when he would find out the truth, or how he would react. And there was always the chance that the playwright had altered the myth and changed things around. Although it knew what to anticipate, the audience wasn't completely sure about what it would get. Even an audience that knew the story had to stay alert.

You're not the same as the Athenians. They saw theatre as part of a religious rite that reaffirmed the basic beliefs of the community. You don't. They brought knowledge with them that you have to get from some clever interpolation by a director. But putting the audience in a privileged seat—that hasn't changed. And your role at the beginning of the play—to become a good detective, using your special knowledge to question, to evaluate, and to anticipate—that hasn't changed either. Even if you've seen the play before, even if you know the ending, you will still get caught up in your role, just like the Athenians.

Hedda's gesture of despair, Mary Tyrone's hands, Willie Loman's exhaustion, the palsied girl's gun, the pre-entrance conversation, and the Greek audience's knowledge are some of the tools playwrights use to start you in your role. Here are more examples from the reigning expert in ways to begin plays, William Shakespeare.

Antony and Cleopatra is a great love story, but it doesn't begin with the lovers. It begins with a speech by a minor character, Philo, to another minor character, Demetrius. It's a speech about thirty seconds long and if you get into your seat a little late, you may think you've missed nothing because Laurence Olivier, or whichever super star is playing Antony this season, has not yet entered.

I had a friend, an English actor, who played Philo in New York when Olivier was playing Antony, and while he was starting up the play he could hear people in the audience (who didn't know the play or what Olivier looked like) whispering to each other: "Is that *him*? Is that *him*?"—and ignoring the speech. Let's quote Philo's speech for those who miss it:

> Nay, but this dotage of our General's
> O'erflows the measure. Those his goodly eyes,
> That o'er the files and musters of the war
> Have glowed like plated Mars, now bend, now turn
> The office and devotion of their view
> Upon a tawny front. His captain's heart,

Which in the scuffles of great fights hath burst
The buckles on his breast, reneges all temper,
And is become the bellows and the fan
To cool a gypsy's lust.

In other words, the Egyptian slut has made a wimp of the Roman general. Is it true? As if on cue, the lovers enter and you get a chance to see for yourself. You'll notice you're not just watching two lovesick people—which is fun for maybe ten seconds. Instead you're thinking: "Did Philo get it right? And how will it affect the love story and the fate of the empire?"

You'll be judging that for the rest of the play, as Antony fights, loves, and makes his choice—the whole known civilized world or one Egyptian Queen. That first little speech of Philo's (try not to miss it) frames the entire play and puts you squarely in your role.

Romeo and Juliet begins with a sonnet by the Chorus:

Two households, both alike in dignity
In fair Verona, where we lay our scene,
From ancient grudge break to new mutiny,
Where civil blood makes civil hands unclean.
From forth the fatal loins of these two foes
A pair of star-crossed lovers take their life,
Whose misadventured piteous overthrows
Doth with their death bury their parents' strife.
The fearful passage of their death-marked love
And the continuance of their parents' rage—
Which but their children's end, naught could remove—

Is now the two-hours' traffic of our stage;
The which if you with patient ears attend,
What here shall miss, our toil shall strive to mend.

Here's the whole story in fourteen lines. Two kids from feuding families meet, love, struggle, die—and that stops the feuding. Obvious audience reaction: "It's nice to be put in a unique position and told what the characters don't know about their fate, but why tell us everything?"

The playwright answers: "I actually haven't told you everything. Many twists and turns to come. But let's face it—watching two kids in love can get cloying pretty fast. On the other hand, if you're aware of their tragic end, then you'll hang on every moment in the story because you know these moments cannot last. And I guarantee that even as you fear the worst, you will still ache with hope that somehow they can avoid their fate."

You have double vision in the theatre. You can know how a play ends, you can know every line of a classic play, and still willingly suspend that knowledge so you can anticipate with hopes and fears and then be surprised. Like a child at bedtime you shiver and say, "Tell me that story again."

By the way, how do you know all this in the first place? The Chorus told you. One moment, please. Up until now we've been assuming that the audience is unseen by the stage. Most audiences prefer the pleasurable fantasy of observing without being observed. It creates a comfortable screen between you and the play. Unlike real life, you—in your privileged seat—are deliciously invisible. You get your information by just happening to see it or overhear it. You get it without being fed it, even though, of course, you actually are being fed it. If you realize the actors are playing to you while pretending to do something else, you're going to get annoyed and you'll fall out of your role.

In the beginning of *Romeo and Juliet* the Chorus addresses you with disarming directness (I know you're there, I'm talking to you.) Also it's in poetry, which provides a screen for the information and makes it a little less direct. It goes down easily.

Plays violating your invisibility to put you in your privileged place are as old as the theatre. The Greeks did it 2,500 years ago with Aeschylus' *The Persians*, which features a chorus of anxious Persian elders addressing the Athenian audience as "ye grave Persians" while waiting for the outcome of the battle of Salamis, which the Athenian audience knew that the Greeks had won and the Persians lost. Today it's common to have someone on the stage talking to you.

But notice how often the "you" is some specialized person you are being asked to become, while the real you remains alert behind your screen of invisibility, evaluating the speaker as well as his words. Peter Shaffer has made an art out of direct address to a specialized you. *Amadeus* begins with an appeal from Salieri, a mediocre eighteenth-century musician (also rumored to have poisoned Mozart), who addresses the audience as "Ghosts of the distant Future," and begs them to "be my confessors!"

This is one more way of giving you the privileged information that starts you in your role of questioning (Who is this guy?), evaluating (Is he sane or crazy?), and anticipating (Does Salieri actually kill Mozart, the innocent genius, who is soon to make his entrance?).

The rule is: At the beginning of the play, the playwright makes sure the audience has knowledge that somebody on the stage does not. No privileged knowledge, no role. But—and this is very important—no matter how cleverly the playwright manages this, you won't stay in your role very long unless you care about the people you're watching. Love them or hate them, you must find something compelling about them.

Who do you care about on the stage? The same people you care about in life: the young, the awkward, the lonely, those who have suffered loss, those who are in conflict, the fish-out-of-water, the brave, the bold, the clever, the venturesome, the good-hearted, and the gallant. Self-pity is off-putting—hard to cry for the one who cries for himself—it steals your role. You enjoy a scoundrel (preferably witty), those who break the rules, those who say what they think, those who deflate the pompous, those who do what you might want to but are afraid to. Also, you may not like but may be fascinated by the inflated, the evil, and even the mean-spirited (if exaggerated and played for laughs).

You care about those who want things and fight for them (especially when they are living illusions and you see the reality). The elephant man wants to be normal. Willie Loman wants the success America promised him. Antony wants Cleopatra (plus the whole world). Romeo and Juliet just want each other and think that love conquers all. Harry Brock is a pirate who thinks he can get anything he wants.

There are people who say, "I only care about people like me." Part of the playwright's job is to get you to feel for people who are not like you, to bridge what you so often find unbridgeable in life. In every well-written play you will find that those you care about are in situations that make them in some way innocent (while you are knowledgeable) and in some way vulnerable (while you in your privileged seat are secure).

The Diary of Anne Frank begins at the end (one more way to place you in your role) with her father re-visiting the attic in Amsterdam where his family hid from the Nazis until they were discovered and sent off to die. He finds his thirteen-year-old daughter's diary. Reading it brings her back again, a young girl awakening to life who doesn't know her fate (as you do). She is both innocent and vulnerable.

But be very careful not to equate innocence with youth and vulnerable with weak.

Othello in Shakespeare's play is no innocent kid in jeopardy. He's a Moorish general, smart, experienced, a leader of men in battle. The playwright demonstrates this early in the play by the good soldierly advice Othello gives to the Venetian Council and the respect they pay him. How can he be an innocent?

Shakespeare lets you know that Othello's a fish-out-of-water. He can't be fooled on the battlefield (where he's spent most of his life); but off the battlefield, in an idle domestic world filled with plots—not much experience there. He doesn't see the threats against him that you do. You're smart, he's...innocent.

And vulnerable too? Well, he lets himself get fooled by his Italian subordinate, Iago, into believing his young wife Desdemona (another innocent) is having an affair with a handsome young officer. Swayed by bogus evidence from a stolen handkerchief, Othello turns madly jealous and strangles her.

Stop for a little problem: Does this sound like innocent and vulnerable?

Or is it more like stupid and cruel? Innocent and vulnerable is what you care about. Stupid and cruel you disdain. Even if innocent in some ways, how can Othello be so badly fooled by Iago and not be thought a dope?

How do you fill the gap between the man you want to like and the action you have to hate? In the twentieth century, starting with Freud, we've developed a consuming interest in motivation—the "why" of things. Maybe Othello is an angry black man in a white world. Maybe he's a middle-aged man worried about declining sexuality. Or maybe—

Elizabethans were much more concerned with getting on with it. For Shakespeare, Othello is a Moor—jealous by nature. Iago is an Italian—crafty by nature. Everybody knows that a crafty Italian can fool a jealous Moor any day.

And why does Iago plot to destroy Othello? Shakespeare says: He's evil. He's a bad guy. No psychology. Then he throws you a bone of motivation. Iago was passed over for promotion and he claims that Othello seduced his wife. (Do you actually believe that? Does anybody? Does Iago?) Is that motivation enough? Need something more these days? Maybe Iago's furious about being a working class guy up from the ranks, surrounded by privileged upper-class twits. Maybe he's bitter about a black man being his superior. Maybe he's worried about his declining sexuality. Or maybe—

Motivation for Shakespeare is something to get over with quickly. Just as he accepted common Elizabethan beliefs about human types (Moors are jealous, Italians are crafty), he used common Elizabethan stage conventions—bad guys fool good guys—otherwise no play.

While twentieth-century heads are trying to make sense of something that cannot be made sense of in twentieth-century terms, the play sweeps you along. You care about Othello. He's innocent and vulnerable. You hate Iago. He's the evil plotter. You love Desdemona. She's the victim. Good people in the grip of evil do bad things. At the end, just before he dies, Othello returns to the noble figure he was, to remind you why you liked him in the first place. As long as the playwright keeps you busy playing your part so you don't have time to ask bad modern questions, the play works fine. As Shakespeare knew, and we sometimes forget, plays are meant to be seen. Some plays deserve study, but almost any play will reveal holes if examined too closely.

Many playwrights deal with people of great sophistication. And yet there is always something innocent about them and some area of vulnerability that they don't see and you do. Henry Higgins, in George Bernard Shaw's *Pygmalion,* is the world's best-educated man. He's teaching Eliza Doolittle, the world's least-educated woman, to speak like a lady. As has been said about Henry Kissinger, Henry Higgins knows everything—but that's all he knows. He knows nothing about the human heart. You can see his emotions are being touched in ways that he does not understand. The world's best-educated man (and arrogant besides) is an innocent. In one crucial area, you're smarter than he is.

Is he vulnerable? Can he suffer loss? Of course he can and he does. He loses the girl in the play (Shaw is a realist). He gets the girl in *My Fair Lady,* the musical based on the play. But he almost loses her and reveals just how vulnerable he is.

If Henry Higgins isn't the world's smartest man, then Oedipus, King of Thebes, is. To gain his kingdom, he had to answer the toughest questions from the sphinx (actually they don't seem so tough, maybe standards were lower then). Now he's searching for the murderer of the previous king, an unpunished criminal who has caused the plague that's killing everyone in the city. Tiresias, a blind prophet, says Oedipus himself is the murderer. Oedipus won't listen. He's arrogant, full of himself. He believes that he (and not the gods) can control life. He's "Oedipus the King, whom all men call great." If you did not know his fate, you might disdain him for his arrogance. Knowing his awful future, you are touched by his innocence and vulnerability.

Oedipus and Henry Higgins are innocent and arrogant. Miranda, in *The Tempest*, is just innocent. She has been so sheltered by her father, Prospero, that she's never seen another man. When she finally meets some pretty ordinary guys, she's stunned and excited. "Oh, brave new world," she says, "that has such creatures in it." You laugh and you love her. So innocent. So vulnerable.

None of these people are weak and stupid. They're often intelligent and strong. But they don't know what you know. They make you feel smart and invulnerable, even godlike.

Tom Stoppard is the most erudite of contemporary playwrights. His characters are often classics-quoting intellectuals. Some theatregoers avoid his plays thinking they won't know enough to understand them. But even Stoppard—or, I should say, especially Stoppard—makes sure that his people are innocent in some way that you are knowledgeable.

In *Arcadia* (1993), two high-powered, quick-thinking, cool-hearted university professors are trying to reconstruct what happened on an estate in Derbyshire in April 1809. One of them believes he's made a fabulous discovery—the real reason Lord Byron left England in 1809. He's found documents that prove (with the help of some creative interpretation) that Lord Byron killed a bad poet in a duel after seducing his wife and writing nasty reviews of his poetry.

It's a clever reconstruction. There should be tons of money in it—power, prestige, a best-selling book, TV talk shows. But it's wrong.

How do you know it's wrong? Well, the playwright helps you out by alternating scenes in the present with scenes from April 1809 that show you facts the literary detectives can only speculate about, putting you one step ahead of them (until the end of the play when you fall one step behind them).

They're smart; you're smarter. They are innocent, not only about the events, but about the hidden feelings of the people on the estate and the unpredictable role love plays in the equations of life—something that you already know and these cool-hearted academics may one day understand.

In *The Invention of Love* (1997), Stoppard presents A. E. Housman, Benjamin Hall Kennedy Professor of Latin at Cambridge University. He's dead (in his case not that much different from being alive)—a dry, friendless scholar, an expert in deciphering two-thousand-year-old Latin love poetry who seems himself devoid of feelings. He looks back on his life as an Oxford undergraduate, where students and professors shared brilliant Latin repartee and a passion for textual criticism.

Heavy going for the theatregoer? Not when you see that Housman is in love with a young student athlete, and is too shy, too innocent, to do anything about it. In a stunning monologue at the end of the first act, Professor Housman, cruel in the classroom toward students whose names he does not remember, brilliantly translates a passionate *Ode* of Horace's and reveals to you—and only you—his despair over himself as a young man who could never find the words for his own passion. You can't quote Horace, but you understand the anguish of tongue-tied love.

Later on, when the truth comes out and his love is not returned, another Housman emerges—A. E. Housman the poet. Only you understand the meaning of the words that find their way into print but that he could never express in life.

Hamlet is the greatest of all Shakespeare's heroes. He not only is young and handsome and strong and witty and intelligent and sophisticated and a good fencer and speaks in iambic pentameter, he's also a prince and a philosopher. True, he's lost his father, he's angry with his mother, and he despises his uncle. But is he an innocent? Is he vulnerable? Yes, to both questions. Let's see how Shakespeare makes it happen.

The play does not start with Hamlet. *Hamlet* starts with a ghost. His dead father, the late king, silent and ominous in his kingly armor, appears to a couple of palace guards and Hamlet's friend Horatio. With this simple move, Shakespeare puts you in your privileged place. Hamlet may be the Prince of Denmark, a prince among princes; nevertheless, for the moment, you know what he doesn't. He is innocent and vulnerable. You don't know why the ghost is there, but you know enough to make you lean forward anticipating what dangerous effects the ghost will have on Hamlet's life.

Hamlet could start without the ghost. You could be surprised along with Hamlet as he goes to meet his dead father and hears his dread command that Hamlet take revenge on his uncle, the murderer, who is now king. Then the earlier scene in the court (act one, scene two), which introduces the major characters, Hamlet, his mother, his uncle the king, the king's counselor, Polonius, and his son Laertes, would be just that— a scene for introducing the characters. You get some information through Hamlet's asides and the first soliloquy. You see his despair over his father's death and his mother's quick remarriage to his uncle. Without your knowledge of the ghost, there's nothing in the scene that helps you question, analyze, or anticipate. Nothing that marks Hamlet as either innocent or vulnerable. And, most important, there's no urgency.

Urgency? What's that?

Urgency is your feeling that right here, right now, something is happening that demands action, something with big potential consequences, something the characters cannot walk away from, and it usually comes with a time limit attached that keeps you glued to the play. You don't know what the ghost wants from Hamlet, but you know that Hamlet cannot run away. He has to meet the ghost now.

It's just after eight o'clock when Thelma Cates, in the opening of 'Night, Mother, finally realizes her daughter Jessie intends to shoot herself in "a couple of hours." If she's going to stop her, she has to do it now.

A country estate is going to be sold to pay the debts of a kind-hearted but improvident family at the opening of Chekhov's The Cherry Orchard. If the estate is to be saved, something must be done now.

At the opening of David Mamet's Glengarry Glen Ross, a fumbling real estate salesman is losing out in a sales contest. The salesman who wins gets a Cadillac. The one who loses gets fired. To save his job, Shelly Levene has to do something now.

Urgencies can appear at different points in a play. Nora Helmer, in the second act of Ibsen's A Doll's House, is threatened by a letter dropped into her husband's mailbox that will expose a harmless fraud she committed years before to raise the money needed to save his health. In a few hours her stiff-necked husband will read the letter. If she's going to save herself she must do something now.

In the third act of *Romeo and Juliet*, Juliet is being forced by her father to marry Paris after she has secretly married Romeo and not at some vague point in the future: "I tell thee what," her father says, "Get thee to church o' Thursday/ Or never after look me in the face." Juliet has to do something and she has to do it now.

Urgency is one of the elements in a play that creates precious moments. From the time the playwright places you in a privileged seat, even if you love the people, the only way the playwright can keep you in your role throughout the play is to make sure that every moment on the stage is a precious moment. This concept is more basic than plot. It determines at which points in people's lives the play will take place.

Precious moments are temporary moments, one-of-a-kind moments, connected to the future by hopes and fears, or put into perspective by looking back at the past. Urgent moments are precious—as are first moments, final moments, moments of threat, testing moments, and stolen moments (people where they shouldn't be, doing what they shouldn't be doing).

In the opening scene of Chekhov's *The Seagull*, Trigorin, a bored writer from the city, encounters Nina, a starry-eyed provincial girl. The first time Trigorin and Nina look at each other, you see the hint of attraction that will create hopes for them and fears for Trigorin's mistress and the boy who loves Nina (who are also mother and son)—a potent first moment.

In the opening scene of Margaret Edson's *Wit* (Pulitzer Prize 1998), Vivian Bearing, in a hospital gown, begins telling you about her life as a cancer patient. She says, "It's not my intention to give away the plot; but I think I die in the end." You hope and fear for her, even as you realize she is narrating her final moments.

In act four of Chekhov's *The Three Sisters*, Tuzenbach, a young army officer who may die in a duel he is about to fight, spends his last threatened moments talking about trees ("I feel elated, I see these fir trees, these maples and birches, as if for the first time..."), while your hopes and fears for him rise.

The most famous stolen moment in the theatre is the kiss between Romeo and Juliet at the Capulets' ball, which seals their love and creates hopes and fears for the young lovers that make you hang on every moment that follows.

Hope and fear always go together in the theatre. If a play moved exclusively in one direction, you would quickly slip out of your role and the moments would cease being precious. Imagine: Romeo and Juliet meet, fall in love, and get married. Ho-hum. Anne Frank is trapped and dies. Sad—too sad to keep you sitting for two hours in a theatre. But Romeo and Juliet are threatened on every side, which creates fear; and Anne Frank, whose death is inevitable, is full of illusions about the future that keep hope alive.

If people on the stage understood everything about their situations from the beginning, either hope or fear would be gone—along with your role. Oedipus refuses to face the truth of Tiresias' prophecies about him by claiming it's all a plot by his brother-in-law Creon. You know better.

Falstaff, in *Henry the Fourth, Part Two*, believes that Prince Hal will continue to love him after he becomes king. He's been thoroughly rejected in the cruelest manner by the new king ("I know thee not, old man"), and yet he turns to his friend Shallow and says: "...Do not you grieve at this. I shall be sent for in private to him." He refuses to give in to his feelings, allowing you to feel for him. Mel Edison, the anxious, depressed executive in Neil Simon's *The Prisoner of Second Avenue*, walks into his apartment which has been ransacked by thieves, turns to his wife and says: "Didn't Mildred come in to clean today?" You laugh and wonder why he doesn't see what you see.

All plays deal with people living their illusions. Let the characters in on the joke and there's no laugh, no tears, no innocence, no vulnerability, and nothing for you to do. It's easy to recognize someone else's illusions; you may not always recognize your own. In the theatre, you are encouraged to have hopes for people you like, no matter what you fear about their futures. By the ends of plays, stage characters change and so do you. Much more about this later.

The purest example I know of a play that makes moments precious is Thornton Wilder's 1938 Pulitzer Prize winner, *Our Town*. The setting is Grover's Corners, a small New Hampshire village at the turn of the twentieth century. The events are the most common happenings in the lives of ordinary people. Almost every moment in the play is made precious by connecting it to the past or the future.

Wilder creates a character called the Stage Manager who appears on an empty stage and introduces the town. He pushes out a couple of tables, a few chairs and a bench. A sound effect or two—a train whistle, a crowing rooster—inspire your imagination.

The Stage Manager is genial, shrewd, a fellow townsman. At the same time he's all-seeing and all-knowing. He connects the town to the recent past. "The earliest tombstones in the cemetery up there on the mountain say 1670–1680—they're Grovers and Cartwrights and Gibbses and Herseys—same names as are around here now." He brings on Professor Willard from the state university to connect the town to the distant past. "Grover's Corners lies on the old Pleistocene granite of the Appalachian range...some of the oldest land in the world."

Playing artfully with time, the Stage Manager looks back at the turn-of-the-century town from the future and gives you information about life and death that no one else has. "There's Doc Gibbs comin' down Main Street now...And here's his wife comin' downstairs to get breakfast...Doc Gibbs died in 1930...Mrs. Gibbs died first—long time ago, in fact...She's up in the cemetery there now..."

When the young newspaper boy appears, the Stage Manager talks about his schooling, his college scholarships and the town's hopes for him, and then almost casually mentions that he will be killed in the Great War. "All that education for nothing."

The Stage Manager shows the audience common experiences seen from multiple perspectives. Against this backdrop, you—and only you—are aware of the fragility of life and the most ordinary moments—a girl and a boy reaching an understanding in a drugstore, a father correcting a boy who's not chopping wood for his mother—become precious. The people in Grover's Corners live by the hopeful optimistic illusions common to everyone. They don't know the realities you know about them—their losses, their sorrows, when they will die. Their urgencies are simple. What's to be done with a drunken church choir director?

And are the two kids about to be married too young and too scared to go through with the wedding?

In the famous first act ending, the Stage Manager connects the moments of life in the town, not to the past or the future, but to the cosmos, and suddenly the smallest things carry the weight of eternity. A boy and his sister look our their window on a moonlit night, and talk about an amazing letter that was addressed to a farm, a village, a county, a state, a country, a continent, a hemisphere, a world, a solar system, and finally the entire universe. "And the postman brought it just the same," says the girl. And the boy says in wonder, "What do you know!"

Finally, and most poignantly, one character looks back at life from the perspective of death. Emily Gibbs, who married George, the boy next door, has died in childbirth. She comes to join the dead in the village graveyard. The dead (sitting in chairs) are indifferent to the living. "Gradually, gradually," says the Stage Manager, "they lose hold of the earth...and the ambitions they had...and the pleasures they had...and the things they suffered...and the people they loved...They get weaned away from earth..."

Emily, still filled with attachments to the living, asks to go back to look at life one last time. She returns to an ordinary day in the past, her twelfth birthday. Seen from the perspective of death, every word, every gesture by her unknowing family is heart-breaking. It is soon too much for her. She has to say good-bye to all the simple pleasures of life. "Clocks ticking...Mama's sunflowers...and food and coffee...and new ironed dresses and hot baths..."

By looking back from the future and ahead from the past, the simplest and most common human experiences have been made precious. It is from these precious moments that the playwright creates his play.

To sum up: At the beginning of a play, the playwright gives you—and only you—knowledge that puts you in a privileged place. Then he gets you into your detective role of questioning, evaluating, and anticipating by using precious moments to convince you that something urgent is happening right here, right now, with hopes and fears for innocent and vulnerable people you care about.

* * *

Part of the playwright's job is to make complicated things seem simple. A play that appears on the stage as a seamless stream of words and actions is made up of many intertwining strands, only some of which we've isolated and discussed. Looking at a few more of these strands will give you a better idea of what the playwright is actually doing and how it affects your role.

I mentioned earlier the scene in *The Elephant Man* in which the hospital nurse brings in the food and then runs screaming from the world's ugliest human. Then I mentioned the other woman, the actress who comes calling and sees the intelligent, sensitive man that you see. These two characters, nurse and actress, are on opposite sides of a divide. One sees the elephant man's outer ugly form, the other sees his inner beauty.

There are two medical men in the hospital, one a surgeon, the other an administrator. In the beginning, both see the elephant man as a disease, though one is kinder than the other. During the course of the play, the surgeon moves from one side of the divide to the other, and sees the elephant man as the actress sees him. Even the elephant man crosses the divide as he learns to appreciate himself. It's as though this play contains two worlds, and everyone on the stage can be placed in one or the other, with major characters moving between them.

Something to think about: If the characters in *The Elephant Man* can be placed into two worlds, is the same true for the characters in other plays? For example, do the characters in *Romeo and Juliet* fall into two worlds? Obvious answer: Romeo and Juliet, Montagues and Capulets, two worlds. It is true that almost everyone in *Romeo and Juliet* is a Montague or a Capulet, but those may not be the two worlds the play has in mind. The Capulets and the Montagues are actually much alike, both look to the past, both are bound by strict rules of family traditions. Both belong in the same world. Remember Mercutio's line as he lies dying: "A plague o' both your houses."

If the Montagues and the Capulets are in the world of tradition, what's the other world and who's in it? There are important people in the play who belong to neither family—Friar Laurence, the nurse, and Mercutio. The friar is not bound by tradition. He bends the rules and marries the young lovers. Juliet's nurse tells Juliet to marry the man her father wants her to marry, even though she's already married to Romeo. Rules mean nothing to her. Mercutio, Romeo's bold and witty friend, is a free thinker. Friendship matters, not tradition. And what about Romeo and Juliet themselves? He's a Montague, she's a Capulet. They have always followed tradition. But remember what Juliet says: "What's in a name? A rose by any other name would smell as sweet." The two young lovers will not be bound by the rules. They will move from one world to the other. Like Friar Laurence, the nurse, and Mercutio, they will live (and die) by their feelings.

A tougher example is Samuel Beckett's *Krapp's Last Tape*. It's a one-character play; how can there be two worlds? Actually there are two characters in the play. There's Krapp, old, constipated, cynical, life down to the lowest ebb, extinguishing with mordant humor any flicker of hope: "All that old misery. Once wasn't enough for you." Then there's the younger self he listens to on tape, pompous, eager, full of passions, hopes, illusions. One world is filled with human juices, which the other world is without.

Briefly noted: In Chekhov's *The Cherry Orchard*, people are divided into those who look back to an aristocratic past or forward to a bourgeois future. By the end of the play, some have stayed behind, some have moved on. All have been changed. Shakespeare's *Antony and Cleopatra* divides people into those with cool rationality, the Romans, and those with wit and sensibility, the Egyptians—hard people and soft people. Antony moves from the Roman world to the Egyptian, with deadly consequences for many. Thornton Wilder divides the people in *Our Town* into the temporary—the living—and the eternal—the dead, and reminds us that in the end everyone moves from the one world to the other.

Can the characters in all plays be divided into two worlds? Try it with some more plays and see if it's true. And if it is true, what difference does it make in your role? You'll have to wait a bit for the explanation, but take my word, it's true and it matters.

A few more points about beginnings: In the very first moment of a play, before anyone appears on the stage, the lights come up on the setting. You look, you blink. This is where it's going to happen? In this place?

Stage settings always use your imagination to connect the seen with the unseen. I've already mentioned the settings in *The Prisoner of Second Avenue* and *Barefoot in the Park*, where what you don't see makes what you do see amusing. In a play by Chekhov, what you see is usually an elderly house in a remote spot in the country—charming maybe, definitely not exciting, often excruciatingly dull. The people in *The Seagull*, *Uncle Vanya*, and *The Three Sisters* feel buried alive in the country. They're filled with touching (and impossible) longings for better lives in other places. The three sisters dream of Moscow, Nina and Konstantin dream of brilliant careers, Uncle Vanya dreams of being someone important, a writer, a philosopher.

Why not set these plays in some other places? Some places more lively where the characters have more of a chance to realize their dreams. What would be lost?

Well, your role for one thing.

If you take the characters out of their dull setting, then there's no longing, no hopes, no illusions. Nothing to put you in your privileged place of seeing in your realistic way what they, in their innocence, do not see. The dull place is often the best place, as long as it's connected to a powerful unseen world.

The old house that stifles people's hopes (and also represents a gracious and cultured way of life) is always threatened by the new world of the vulgar and the ambitious. Natasha, the bourgeois social climber in *The Three Sisters*, appears from that other world to marry the brother, Andrei, and gradually forces the sisters out of their home. In *The Cherry Orchard* the house is a refuge from the new world, represented by Lopakhin, the emerging capitalist, who will buy the house and the cherry orchard and take an ax to them to make way for summer cottages. The house in *Uncle Vanya* is not only menaced by the professor who wants to sell it, but by the unseen farmers and timber cutters who are destroying the countryside. Outside the old house, ideas from a new world are creating waves that will deeply affect the people in these rooms, leading some to despair and some to new hope. Chekhov's threatened houses are the metaphor for the destruction of one world by another. Note: Not just two worlds, but one world under siege by another. Later on, you will see how these clashing worlds and the movement of characters between them affect your role.

One final point: The beginning of a play announces the universe of the play, not just the visual setting, but the interior geography, the logic, the ground rules. In each play you enter a different universe. Sometimes it seems more or less like the universe you live in. Sometimes it's an obviously different place. You may not know how to express it, but it's clear that Ionesco inhabits a different universe than Neil Simon or Sophocles or Tennessee Williams or Shakespeare.

Nevertheless, you always begin your audience role with a bit of tension and a need for orientation: "Where am I? What are the rules here? Is it okay to laugh?"

Audiences always come ready to be amused, so plays often begin with something funny that sets a kind of baseline. The playwright doesn't want you to laugh at the serious. If he can get you to recognize comedy at the beginning, then when he gets more sober you'll see the contrast. *This* is funny, *that* is serious.

Tony Kushner's *Angels in America* (Pulitzer Prize 1993) begins with a funeral. An elderly rabbi is speaking over the coffin of an elderly woman who died in an old people's home. He says what elderly rabbis often say: He did not know the deceased, but her life represented something larger than herself. He connects her with the Great Voyages made by immigrants to America that cannot be repeated and yet still exist in their descendants. In them is an ancient culture from which they cannot escape.

What universe is this? And where's the funny part? Well, the rabbi jokes about the gentile names (a hint of corruption) of the old woman's grand-children—a theme not unheard of in real-world Jewish funerals. But there is something odd (and amusing and strange) in the scene. Behind the rabbi's long gray beard (an obvious fake), you think you see (and you know you hear) a woman. *The old Jewish rabbi is being played by a woman with a false beard.* What to make of this? A shortage of actors? Bad work in the hirsute department?

Remember, this is the first scene of the play. Surely in a large cast there's a man who can do the part. Maybe Tony Kushner's universe is not quite our universe. Maybe it's a tricky place, a witty place, a vaudeville type of place, a place of theatrical possibilities.

Scene two is a realistic scene with a gleefully corrupt Jewish lawyer and an honest naïve Mormon law clerk. The lawyer is Roy Cohn, a histor-ical figure; the Mormon is a fictional character. Roy Cohn is on the telephone, cursing, browbeating, stealing, bribing, giving and getting favors. In between calls, he offers the law clerk a job in Washington with the attorney general (a favor that will have to be paid back one day). He takes a moment from chicanery to present his vision of a vicious soulless world in which he revels. Again, a scene has expanded from the personal to the global, and in both scenes there is the sense of decay and moral corruption.

This theme of a decaying world is picked up in scene three. A Mormon woman (wife of the Mormon law clerk) is having a pill-induced fantasy. She imagines looking down at the whole earth and seeing the ozone layer poisoning the atmosphere. Again the play is expanding its reach, from individual misery to apocalyptic visions of collapse, and also expanding its theatrical reach, from reality to fantasy.

Each scene that follows continues linking the fate of an individual to the theme of general collapse using different techniques to dramatize it. In scene four, a gay kid with AIDS describes his condition and his fears, and you feel the growing worldwide plague.

Scene five is split: The Jewish lover of the AIDS victim talks to the rabbi about historical processes, specifically the neo-Hegelian sense of positive historical progress, which makes it hard for him to deal with sickness— a cover story to justify leaving his sick friend because he's scared for himself. At the same time, the Mormon law clerk talks to his wife about going to Washington to become part of something larger than himself—in this case the Reagan administration, which he sees as having restored truth and goodness to American life. His wife sees him hiding his sexual problems behind his big thoughts. She knows the world is coming to an end.

The universe of the play continues to stretch. It descends in the next scene to the men's toilet in the courthouse where the AIDS victim's lover spots the Mormon as another gay guy, and then expands again into a scene of the AIDS victim and the Mormon wife, strangers to each other, invading each other's dreams. The wife points out there's no way this can be happening—and yet it is. They tell each other truths. They see each other on the edge of revelation.

Kushner's universe is not limited by psychology, realism, past or future. Rules? None. Subject matter: Everything. It keeps expanding the believable, opening the canvas, making it acceptable for a sex-starved woman to suddenly think about global poisoning, or for a rabbi to have a fake beard, or for an angel to crash through a ceiling. And you never stop to say, "I don't believe that." Or, "I don't believe this person would talk like that." It's a free-spirited, free-wheeling universe that you accept easily.

Next time you're in the theatre, you might notice the moment where you begin to relax as you say to yourself, "Ah, it's *that* kind of play!"

* * *

We've been pulling plays apart and examining the pieces. Now let's stitch one back together, breathe a bit of life into it, and see in some detail how your role develops over a whole act.

Brian Friel's 1980 drama *Translations* is set in a "hedge-school" in an unused barn in County Donegal, Ireland. The year is 1833. Looking back from your privileged seat over a hundred and fifty years later, you know before the play starts that the way of life you're going to see is long gone. The playwright's task is to present a rural Irish world (most of which you only imagine) and make it appear sturdy, even timeless, while setting in motion the forces that will destroy it—forces which, at the very beginning, only you seem to notice.

It's late afternoon. Students are gathering in the barn after working in the fields and the turf banks. Manus, the schoolmaster's lame son, is trying to get Sarah, a mute Irish girl, to say her name. Meanwhile, Jimmy Jack, a shabby elderly worker, quotes Latin and Greek classics. There's an amusing contrast between who he is and what he studies. Friel comments in his stage directions: "*For Jimmy Jack, the world of the gods and the ancient myths are as real and immediate as everyday life in the townland of* Baile Beag." Or, as Jimmy Jack himself says: "Homer knows it all."

Notice, as part of playwright tactics, how characters are paired. Jimmy Jack, the most erudite student, is introduced as a counterpoint to Sarah who can barely speak. The playwright constructs his universe out of contrasts and comparisons so you can make quick judgments about people. It's not a novel—no turning back and no stopping to reflect in the theatre. A play may contain many subtleties, but they have to rest on broad firm limbs. How do you decide quickly that someone is smart? The playwright shows you dull. How do you know someone is beautiful? The playwright shows you plain. (In Hollywood movies, the beautiful leading lady always has a plain best friend.)

Another student appears, Maire, a strong young farm girl, coming from a day of harvesting. She is quick and aggressive where Sarah is slow and passive. Sarah worships Manus, gives him flowers. Maire likes Manus, but not as much as Manus likes her. He seems indecisive, while she is up and doing, ambitious, ready to take action.

Maire and Jimmy exchange words in Latin about the harvest. Maire concludes by saying: "That's the height of my Latin. Fit me better if I had even that much English." This strikes you as odd. After all, English is what she's speaking. Jimmy continues, saying to Maire: "English? I thought you had some English?"

It dawns on you that they aren't speaking English. They're speaking Irish, which you are hearing as English. A little surprising when you're supposed to be in your privileged place of knowledge, but a charming surprise because it makes you smarter than you thought you were. They're speaking Irish and you understand it.

Maire tries out her one line of English. She says it strangely because she's speaking a foreign language she doesn't understand. "In Norfolk we besport ourselves around the maypoll."

You laugh at Maire because you understand what she doesn't, and you realize that the comedy has taught you the language ground rules of the play. Greek is heard as Greek, Latin is heard as Latin, but Irish is heard as English, with the exception of Irish place names, which are heard as Irish. English is one language the students don't understand. Manus the teacher understands a little. Not logical but it doesn't have to be. It's like one of those World War II refugee movies in which everyone speaks English with different accents, except here the one language they don't understand is the one language they are speaking. Complicated to think about, and yet your imagination accepts the premise easily. Language— its importance and its limits—is what the play is about. Language as communication and miscommunication. Language giving us our identity. Language trapping us, language freeing us. Language as battleground. For now, the important point is that you—and only you—understand everybody. This gives you a unique relationship to the stage.

While they wait for the schoolmaster who is off drinking somewhere, Manus tells Maire about a letter he wrote for an old lady who dictated a diatribe against the drunken schoolmaster and his lame son running a hedge-school and wasting people's time and money. They laugh (you do too) about the old lady's stupidity (she forgot Manus is the lame son), and then she added: "Thank God one of them new national schools is being built." For one moment, the hedge-school that seems so permanent is suddenly threatened. They don't seem to notice; you do.

Two more students enter, and with them comes the shadow of a more particular threat. Maire has already mentioned the English soldiers below in the tents, coming to give them a hand with the harvest. "I don't know a word they're saying, nor they me; but sure that doesn't matter, does it?" An alert goes off in your head. When a stage character says something doesn't matter, you can bet it does. In a play about language, every note of non-communication is full of threat.

Bridget, who is young and brash, and Doalty, a loutish witty farmer, enter and the threat becomes more distinct. Doalty reports "the red coats" are doing something with chains and a big machine at the foot of *Cnoc na Mona* that the Irish don't understand. The name of the machine, theodolite, is a subject for an etymological hunt and one of Doalty's practical jokes. He's moving the chains and confusing the British. The chains make you think of shackles. Your imagination takes a leap: a land in shackles. It's deadly serious to you, but the students laugh. Grim humor from a conquered people without weapons. Doalty mimics the soldiers speaking that stupid language, English. It sounds like gibberish to him. It may remind you how easy it is to dehumanize others you don't understand.

They turn quickly to talk of farming and local gossip. Jimmy looks to Virgil for advice about planting corn. No one seems equipped to deal with present dangers. They seem in another world—so innocent, so vulnerable—except for Manus who speaks of Doalty's practical joke as a "gesture." This remark only emphasizes his helplessness, leaving you to feel that ominous shadows are hovering over people who don't seem to be responding. You want to call down to the stage: "Pay attention! Something's happening!"

Today, all these people and their way of life are long gone. You may be watching their last precious moments. All were innocent. All were vulnerable. All had hopes. All were threatened. Do you care about them? Yes. Not because they ask for your sympathy, but because they don't. This allows you your role of feeling for them.

But there is no urgency. Nothing yet to make you tense up in your seat.

Then comes the first moment that changes everything, that alerts you and gives you the first whiff of the possibility of urgency. The interesting thing about this moment is that it's a moment of silence. Manus, trying to get the class started, asks about two absent students. "What about the Donnelly twins? Are the Donnelly twins not coming anymore?" Doalty, the class clown, to whom the question is addressed, turns away without answering. Curious. Doalty always has a lot to say. Manus goes on: "Did you ask them?" Doalty says: "Haven't seen them. Not about these days." Strange abrupt answer from a talkative jokester. Stranger still, Doalty starts whistling through his teeth. You watch and think, "Now what's that all about?" And then the playwright inserts a stage direction (which you won't read, but you'll surely notice): "*Suddenly the atmosphere is silent and alert.*"

One of the many tasks of a playwright at the beginning of a play is to set the rules of the universe he's presenting. Rules of logic, rules of style, rules of behavior that set the tone of the play. As you watch, you won't be categorizing the rules consciously, but you will sense them. And you'll be aware when they're being violated. The world of the hedge-school (especially before the master arrives) is easy going, witty, and garrulous. These people enjoy talking. When they all fall silent, you hear that silence.

In life, of course, you'd never notice. Life's too messy. In the theatre every word, every gesture, every sound counts, because all the irrelevant words, gestures, and sounds are left out. The most potent sound effect—sudden silence—coming out of a background of talk, makes you sit up alertly: What's happening here?

Consider Doalty's whistling through his teeth. Could it be a signal? To the others? To keep quiet? Doalty, who plays tricks on British soldiers just for the fun of it, now shows unanticipated depth. Indeed, there's a sudden sense of secrets shared all around. These simple-minded country people, seemingly ignorant of the threats that surround them, know something. And you don't.

Wait a second. You're in your privileged seat of knowledge. You're in your role, ahead of the game, seeing more than they do. Suddenly—with a whistle and a surprise moment of silence—you've fallen behind. Bit of a jolt there.

Ah, but you do know something. You've caught a clue. Your mind is working, and your role is changing from comfortable know-it-all to detective on the trail of understanding.

Back to the play: After a couple more questions and inconclusive answers about the Donnelly twins, brash Bridget says, out of nowhere, that "two of the soldiers' horses were found last night at the foot of the cliffs at *Machaire Buide* and—" She stops. She won't say anymore. She's said enough. You connect the whistle, the silence, the absent Donnelly twins, the dead horses. Threats are out there. Violence is in the air.

There's a hint of action—the British are up to something; and a hint of counter-action—a few of the Irish are doing something about it. You are catching up to the students, and you appear to be ahead of Manus, the teacher, who seems to notice nothing. Before he seemed the most aware, now he seems the least.

There are always different levels of understanding in a play. There is always somebody on the stage who knows less than you. For you to feel knowledgeable, someone else has to be ignorant. That keeps you in your role. You are the evaluator, the good detective. You are piecing things together on your own, no one telling you anything, no one spoon-feeding you. You feel pretty smart in the theatre.

But you have not yet reached the end of the beginning of the play. There are suggestions of more threats: potatoes may be rotting, famine may loom. More hints about British intent: in the new national free school only English will be taught. No room for a hedge-school where students pay to learn in Irish. So their language is in jeopardy, which means their culture, their very identity. Personal relationships are strained—Maire is leaving for America, to get ahead in life; Manus is staying, unable to act. Family relationships are strained—Manus and his father may want the same job at the national school. Every aspect of their lives—personal, familial, romantic, educational, cultural, political, economic, something as simple as getting enough to eat, or as complex as culture and identity, their future, even their past—all this is in jeopardy and they don't seem to grasp it. They spend their time on etymology and classical languages and gossip. Of course, there are the Donnelly twins, unseen and menacing in the background, but mainly they live on illusions and a kind of fatalism—life will go on no matter what. Only you, the realist, see how fragile it all is.

One thing is still missing. There's still no concrete urgency that makes you lean forward in your seat. No answer yet to the unstated questions that every audience asks of every play at the beginning: "Why here? Why now?"

The schoolmaster enters, as anticipated. Well, almost. Nothing in a play ought to happen exactly as you think it will. Everything should hit with a bit of surprise. So, just when they think the master isn't coming, he enters, arriving from the christening of a new baby. He's alcoholic, imperious, erudite, filled with love for learning, love of words, of the history of words, of knowledge for its own sake. He's lovingly presented, this teacher of the skills and the languages of the past, made poignant by all you know of the threats to his fragile world. English is invading. He jokes about the English language with easy-going contempt ("Good for commerce"). Maire wants to learn it, so she can go to America. The master ignores her. His mind is in the past. He seems unaware, or unable to do anything about the threats that are out there, growing larger but still vague and unformed, not yet with the sharp edge of urgency that makes you begin to anticipate with hopes and fears.

Then a new character is introduced, unprepared for, a surprise, framed in the doorway of the school. It's the master's other son, Owen— charming, enthusiastic, successful, decent, at ease with himself (in contrast with his intense though impotent brother). He's gone to Dublin, he's successful, he speaks English, and he's back. He looks around the school and says happily, "Nothing's changed!" You know when a character says, "Nothing's changed!" everything is going to change. And from the moment you see him, you know he brings urgency with him, but it's urgency in a subtle, almost benign shape.

Owen introduces two English officers, his "friends." They've come to talk to the people and explain what they're doing. The playwright likes to bring in his characters in pairs, and here they are: the cartographer, Captain Lancey, in charge of mapping the land, and the orthographer, Lieutenant Yolland, in charge of naming the places. One an engineer, dry, no feelings, not good with words, who thinks of the Irish (if he thinks of them at all) as children. The other one a dreamer, all feelings, who loves the people, the landscape, and the names. (The irony is he's come to change those names). So, a two-headed enemy. But nobody's bad, nobody's evil. The English are doing their job—making new maps of the land and "regularizing" the names (i.e., putting them in English), and Owen's there to be their go-between and translator, as they begin destroying a language. Urgency has arrived, right here, right now, and it speaks English. And who understands English? You do.

Consider what's happening: English soldiers and Irish farmers (each speaking their own language) do not understand each other. Since Irish is heard as English and English is heard as English, you understand everyone. They don't know it, but they are all speaking English. This simple theatrical conceit gives you—in your privileged place—godlike powers. You—and only you—can see the slights, the threats, the generosities, the misconceptions, the understandings without words, the misunderstandings with words.

How often in life can you sit unobserved and understand perfectly two people who don't understand each other? What powers you have in the theatre! You can smile at the erudite Irish who try to find a common language with the English—perhaps Latin? Smile at Captain Lancey, the ignorant, superior Englishman, who takes Latin for Gaelic, neither of which he understands, nor cares to understand. Smile at Owen's deliberate mistranslations, as he softens Lancey's military speech and then encourages the awkward Yolland by telling him Maire is "dying to hear you speak." You in the audience understand so much (you're really in your role now), you start to anticipate, to predict: There's going to be a clash here. People are going to get hurt. But there's much you don't know yet that will take you by surprise.

So here are two worlds engaged on the battlefield of language: The past and the future. The poetic and the practical. The Irish and the English. It's not quite that simple. Maire who is Irish wants to learn English and get away to America. The Englishman Yolland is in love with Ireland and wants to stay and learn the language. Owen has sympathy for his own people, but he lives and prospers in the other world.

Perhaps it's a clash between two attitudes rather than between two peoples. Even if you can't pin it down simply, you'll identify easily which characters are in which world, and which ones are moving between them. All drama, as you'll soon see, involves people from one world entering another.

For now, just notice one of the most charming and touching dialogue exchanges at the end of the beginning of this play. It's a moment to treasure. And it's a moment that only you will appreciate. After Owen has explained to his father, his brother, and the students about the Englishmen waiting to talk to them, he notices Sarah, the young woman who was mute at the start of the play.

> OWEN: That's a new face. Who are you?
> SARAH: My name is Sarah.
> OWEN: Sarah who?

Sarah: Sarah Johnny Sally.

Owen: Of course! From *Bun na hAbhann*! I'm Owen—Owen Hugh Mor. From *Baile Beag*. Good to see you.

Look at the stage picture: Sarah, who has just learned to speak her own language, and Owen, the translator, who is helping to destroy it. The names —*Bun na hAbhann, Baile Beag*—ordinary to them, mysterious and magical to you, are soon to be extinguished. It's a moment that means little to the people themselves; to you—the audience—filled with foreboding about what is going to happen, it is haunting and heartbreaking. Now, every time you hear an Irish place name, you know it's going to be lost, along with another piece of these people, their past, their culture. You care for them desperately, and you want to shout down at them, "Don't let this happen!"

Very seldom in life do you sense a precious moment actually taking place. Here it is for you, and nobody has to tell you about it or explain it. It's for moments of exquisite understanding like this that you go to the theatre.

Manus, who understands English, has heard enough to know what is happening. Owen knows, but doesn't seem to care. The schoolmaster, Hugh ought to know, but he's drunk. The others, the students, how aware are they of the threat? Some of them—Doalty and Bridget— know something. You're not sure how much. Some of them, like the shadowy Donnelly twins, may be taking action. One thing is certain— if everybody understood what you understand and talked openly about it, there would be no role for you. The playwright has to leave a space for you to play your part. You fear for those who can't, won't, or don't know enough to fear for themselves. As playwrights have all discovered, characters who moan and groan for themselves are off-putting. Better for them to smile and you to worry.

Manus, who knows more than he has let on, tries to make it clear for Owen. The English have come with a military operation. Everything Irish is to be eliminated. The English have even eliminated Owen's name. They call him Roland. "It's only a name," says Owen, refusing to be alarmed. You know what's in a name. People get killed over a name.

A large outer story has been set in motion. One world is under siege by another. What will be the consequences? This could be the end of the act, but it's not.

Manus watches as Owen takes Maire by the hand and introduces her to Lt. Yolland. A young man and a young woman, one English one Irish, look at each other. Something unspoken may be happening between them. You see it. Does Manus see it? And what will he do about it? Thus a smaller inner story is set in motion.

I've suggested that there are two worlds in every play. Here's a new thought: Almost every play contains two stories, one inner and one outer. Understanding the interplay between them will be your work in the next act. But don't worry, the playwright will do most of the heavy lifting for you.

The play has begun. Something urgent is threatening innocent and vulnerable people. The playwright gives you a godlike view. Unlike God, you don't know what's going to happen next.

First Intermission

We have ten minutes; want to stretch your legs? Let me buy you a drink and I'll tell you a story.

I met Joe Kramm in 1952. I remember the date because I had come to New York on my honeymoon and my great aunt Nelise Child, the playwright (you've never heard of her), threw a party for us in her big old apartment on Central Park West.

Lots of celebrities were on hand. Famous songwriters, famous directors (the young Hal Prince was there), many others whose names I've forgotten. The star of the party, the one everybody lingered around, the one on whom all the lights seemed to shine, was Joe Kramm.

"Who"—I can hear you saying—"is Joe Kramm?" In 1952, Joe Kramm was the king of New York playwrights. His play had just won the Pulitzer Prize. Remember? No? It was a play called *The Shrike*. Remember now? It was about a man trapped in a psychiatric ward by an estranged wife determined to get him back. Harrowing melodrama. Made Uta Hagen a star. Became an excellent movie. Even today, you might actually see it once every couple of years at three o'clock in the morning on local TV.

Joe Kramm turned out to be a very nice guy—barely middle-aged, good looking, pleasant, very approachable. I was just twenty-four, with no idea what I wanted to do with my life. He told me about *The Shrike* (my great aunt, he said, had supplied the title). He talked about his new play that was called (I never forgot this): *The Gypsies Wore High Hats*. It was in rehearsal, soon to go into previews and then open on Broadway. I said to myself, "You know, I think I'd like to do something like that."

I did not see Joe Kramm again for sixteen years. In 1968, my first play opened in New York at Lincoln Center. My great aunt Nelise gave a dinner party for me, and Joe Kramm was there. She was especially happy to see him because he rarely appeared in public anymore. *The Gypsies Wore High Hats* had never opened on Broadway. It had closed in previews. His wife, an actress, had died on stage while performing in *The Shrike*. The play was still being done occasionally, on college campuses and in tiny theatres.

Joe had never gotten another play on Broadway. He lived in a furnished room. He never read the newspapers, never went to the theatre. This night was an occasion for him. He talked—a little too insistently—about the prizes he had won and the honors he'd been given. He was tired looking, pasty faced. He said he was working on an autobiographical novel. It was a big project; he didn't know when it would be finished. A couple of years later he was dead. Got a small obit in the *Times*.

Today, Joe Kramm is totally unknown. His famous play is never performed. It's an unusual person who remembers his name. Well, styles change. Only the rare play retains its freshness and sense of rightness for more than a season or two. Who lately has seen the plays of John Van Druten, S. N. Behrman, Robert Sherwood, Sherwood Anderson, Elmer Rice?

Writing a play is very tough. You get an idea in one year, start it the next, finish it the next. If you're lucky it gets a reading and maybe, in a couple more years, a production. If you're very lucky it actually gets to Off-Broadway, and if you're super lucky—you get the idea. Then the reviewers yawn through it and say: "Too bad. Last year's." Or they scratch their heads and you say: "Too bad. Next year's." Once in a great while, it's well-cast, well-directed, catches the front of the wave, and suddenly you're king for a moment.

What's the point? It's only a play. But there is something magical about getting an audience to respond—to laugh when you want them to laugh, cry when you want them to cry, imagine when you want them to imagine, even think when you want them to think. That never happens in real life. And I love it.

Oh, my 1968 play at Lincoln Center? It failed. But like the homely guy who won't stop chasing the girls, I kept at it, hoping to get lucky one day.

The house lights are blinking. Finish your drink and we'll go back in.

Middles

Back in your privileged seat, you're ready for the next act. You've done well in your detective role. You've met the people, learned the ground rules of their universe, placed them in two worlds, seen them enter two stories—one inner, one outer. You know what they want. You see the threats they don't. You're anticipating. You feel the urgency. You care. Let's get on with it.

The play continues where you left it—just as clever as before, the characters as compelling, the laughs as big, the relationships as potent, the urgency as urgent. And yet, and yet...something is not quite right. You feel it, even if you can't say what it is. You clear your throat. You shift in your seat. You—God forbid—look at your watch. You're still in your role, but the electric tension that made you focus totally on the stage in the first act has gone slack. If asked to explain what you feel, you may shake your head and say, "I don't know, it's just not going anywhere."

The middle is the tricky part. This is where new plays often crumble and audiences find themselves examining the proscenium sculptures and the exit signs. But before you leave, mentally or physically, let's freeze the action on the stage and consider what should be happening in the middle of a play that will keep you in it.

First, a quick spell-check. I'm a really bad speller. For years I thought I was a "p-l-a-y-w-r-i-t-e." Sounds reasonable—someone who writes plays—but it's wrong. I'm a "p-l-a-y-w-r-i-g-h-t."

What's a "w-r-i-g-h-t"? There are iron wrights, wheelwrights, and ship-wrights. These are workers who shape hard materials to fit designs. Exactly what a playwright does, except we call our designs "structures," or "actions."

One can be a great playwright without being a great writer. O'Neill showed us that. Or one can be an elegant writer and a poor playwright. Henry James comes to mind. Aristotle in *The Poetics*, notes that there can be "drama with action and no characters, but not with characters and no action." No matter how brilliant a writer is, if he/she cannot build a proper structure, he/she is not a playwright.

Pause for a moment to consider the kind of structure we're discussing. A wheel has structure. Also a ship, a bridge, a building, a painting. All these structures have something in common. They are structures in space. A play is different. Aristotle, in a famous passage, says, "A play has a beginning, a middle, and an end." That is to say, a play is a structure in time. A film is a structure in time. A novel is a structure in time. Music is structure in time. (Yes, there are time considerations in art and architecture, the progress of the eye around a composition, and there are spatial considerations in theatre—stage pictures—but let's keep to the main points.)

It takes only a small amount of experience to realize that it's harder to conceptualize a structure in time than a structure in space. You can visu-alize Yankee Stadium, a structure in space, a lot easier than you can visualize a baseball game, a structure in time. But even in baseball the structure is the same in each game and you get a chance to think about it after every inning. And if you don't understand a passage in a novel you can read it over again. A play (like a film) is a structure in time meant to be grasped in one continuous viewing, no turning back, and no instant replay. Sounds difficult, doesn't it? And yet, ordinary people do it every night.

There's a curious corollary to this. While a play is a structure in time, and the passage of time is one of the most poignant parts of any drama (temporary moments are precious moments), few clocks are found on the stage. Think about the last play you saw that had a clock in it, or where one character asked another for the time. (Unless time plays a specific role, as in Marsha Norman's 'Night, Mother where Jessie Cates promises to kill herself in two hours and the kitchen clock becomes the point of urgency.)

Question: If the passage of time is so basic to the structure of a play, why aren't there clocks on the stage? Let's put one on the stage and see what happens.

Ibsen's A Doll's House begins with Nora coming home on the afternoon of December 24th with gifts and tree decorations. Let's start the clock at 3:00 p.m. For a few minutes Nora talks to her husband about happy days to come now that he's been promoted to bank manager. At 3:05, two guests appear—one expected, a doctor who's a family friend, and one unexpected, a woman Nora hasn't seen for many years. 3:06: While the doctor goes to visit Nora's husband in the next room, the woman tells Nora about her sad life and asks for help in getting a job at the bank. 3:14: A disreputable man who works at the bank enters. Nora's friend recognizes him as someone from her past.

3:16: The doctor appears from the next room to say nasty things about the disreputable man who's gone in to see Nora's husband. 3:18: The husband appears and says the disreputable man has left, and yes there is now a vacant position at the bank that can be filled by Nora's friend. 3:20: The husband, the doctor, and Nora's friend leave. 3:21: Nora's children enter and play with her.

3:22: The disreputable man reappears. Nora's husband has fired him. He pleads with Nora for help and, when she refuses, reminds her that he was the one who secretly loaned her the money for her husband's trip to Italy that restored him to health after an illness. Furthermore, he accuses Nora of signing her dead father's name to satisfy the legal requirements for the loan. Unless she helps him now, he will tell all, and she will be disgraced and jailed as a forger. 3:34: The disreputable man leaves and Nora decorates the Christmas tree. 3:35: Nora's husband enters and talks about the disreputable man who had to be fired because he was once a forger and forgers poison all life. End of act: 3:40.

This gives you an idea of how much can happen in a woman's life in forty minutes on the stage. Watching it you don't think about the time, especially since you're in the hands of a playwright who makes everything seem reasonable. If there was a clock suspended above the action, all those quick comings and goings could make an Ibsen drawing room seem like a busy railroad station. And compared with forty minutes in your own life, it might even appear—and this would kill the play— unbelievable.

A Doll's House is one of those plays with ground rules of human activity that seem roughly like our own. But even the most naturalistic play would appear strange and artificial if the author allowed too close a comparison with real life. Stage time and real time are quite different. Ten minutes on the stage can feel like a half hour. The stage eliminates all our chitchat—the hellos and good-byes, the repetitions and the irrelevancies that make up so much of life. Therefore, a playwright trying to give his play the impression of a naturalistic surface will eliminate ordinary frames of reference, like clocks.

Some plays make no attempt at realism. *Oedipus the King* has a very artificial surface. In the course of an hour and fifteen minutes of continuous action, a delegation begs Oedipus to figure out the source of the plague that's killing people in his city, while at the same time his brother-in-law Creon returns from the oracle to announce that the plague is caused by the unavenged murder of the previous king. Oedipus curses the killer and promises to find him. A blind prophet accuses Oedipus himself of being the killer (and worse), which Oedipus refuses to believe. As he presses forward in his investigation, a messenger and a shepherd reveal that Oedipus is both the lost son of the murdered king and the murderer, and has married his own mother and is the source of the plague. The queen, his mother/wife kills herself. Oedipus pokes out his own eyes. His brother-in-law Creon will be the new king. His kids—Well, you can imagine.

Compare this with the busiest hour and a quarter in your life and it would seem—admit it—a little silly. Even if you accept the speeches of the chorus as a device to create transitions in time, it's still a pretty crowded schedule for one day in the life of a king—if you count the hours. But who's counting? You aren't. You're playing your role in a ritual tragedy.

Playwrights know that audiences will accept almost any "given" at the beginning of a play. Why not? You've paid your money, you've sat down in this neutral space, you're eager to enter the playwright's universe. You would not be pleased if anything like a clock pulled you away.

Shakespeare's *Othello* appears to have two time schemes: one to concentrate time, one to spread time. General Othello, newly married to

Desdemona, a young and beautiful Venetian, goes to Cyprus as military commander. In what seems like an intense couple of days, his evil under-officer, Iago, convinces him that his wife is sleeping with Cassio, a young captain, which drives Othello to murder.

In the second time scheme, there are many hints that Othello has spent far longer on the island, giving Iago the opportunity to produce enough "proofs" of a long affair. For example, Iago claims he will get Cassio to admit "Where, how, how oft, how long ago, and when/ He hath and is again to cope your wife." Some of Iago's plottings (like arranging for Othello to see Desdemona's handkerchief in Cassio's hands) are awfully complex to have been organized in a few hours. And how could any man be driven from loving husband to murderer in a couple of days? You would need two clocks to time this play, and watching them simultaneously would drive you crazy.

Graduate students pouring over the text can spend weeks sorting all this out. And yet, no one who goes to see *Othello* on the stage is the least bit confused. And no one in the audience ever stops to ask how long Othello has been on that island or exactly how long it takes for Iago to drive him crazy. (A lot of playwright technique is designed to keep you from asking bad questions.)

Shakespeare stretches or condenses time as needed by eliminating both clocks and calendars. He can make time slow down, as when Romeo and Juliet first speak to each other using the exquisite formality of a sonnet.

> **ROMEO:** If I profane with my unworthiest hand
> This holy shrine, the gentler sin is this:
> My lips, two blushing pilgrims, ready stand

To smooth that rough touch with a tender kiss.
JULIET: Good pilgrim, you do wrong your hand too much,
Which mannerly devotion shows in this.
For saints have hands that pilgrims' hands do touch,
And palm to palm is holy palmers' kiss.
ROMEO: Have not saints lips, and holy palmers, too?
JULIET: Ay, pilgrim, lips that they must use in prayer.
ROMEO: Oh then, dear saint, let lips do what hands do:
They pray; grant thou, lest faith turn to despair.
JULIET: Saints do not move, though grant for prayers' sake.
ROMEO: Then move not while my prayer's effect I take.

Followed by a kiss, which seals their fate. Later, at the end of the balcony scene, Shakespeare can even make time stand still. As Romeo is leaving, Juliet calls to him to ask about their next meeting, and then says: "I have forgot why I did call thee back." Romeo says: "Let me stand here till thou remember it." A tiny pause, you hold your breath. You don't want this moment to end. Juliet says: "I shall forget, to have thee still stand there, /Rememb'ring how I love thy company." And Romeo answers: "And I'll still stay, to have thee still forget..."

For a few moments, time stops. Truffaut did it with stop-motion photography. Shakespeare does it with words.

The playwright wants you to be aware of time. He does not want you thinking too accurately about it. He wants no awkward comparisons between his universe and yours. He wants to release you from anything that could disturb the ground rules he has established. Therefore, no clocks. But by the middle of the performance a playwright must have you believing that the play is moving purposefully through time, that it is "going somewhere."

How does he do this? First, by getting you to concentrate, not on clocks, but on process.

Back to *A Doll's House*. Nora enters on December 24th and starts to decorate a Christmas tree. In the second act, the tree is bare, with one burned out candle. The passage of time is human and natural—tree decorated, tree empty. Candles burned imply candles lit. That was the day before Christmas, this is Christmas day. You're in your role of detective, you catch on quickly. You won't focus consciously on these things and yet they give a sense of time passing that encourages you to believe the melodramatic events in the foreground of the play.

There are other kinds of human and natural processes that deliver the sense of life progressing. Some plays start in the morning and end at night. Some plays start in one season with trees blooming, and end in another season with trees bare. Some plays start with a crime, move to investigation, finish with a trial. Some plays show characters growing up, getting married, growing old.

Time seems to stand still in Chekhov's *The Three Sisters*, but years are passing. People fall in and out of love. Dreams get eaten up. The sisters don't go to Moscow, they get jobs. Soldiers, who seemed such a permanent part of their lives, leave. Their brother has a lady friend, gets married, has children, and takes over their house.

Some plays exaggerate the passage of time for comedy. Millions of years pass between the acts of Thornton Wilder's *The Skin of Our Teeth*. There are cataclysmic changes—all of natural evolution in a couple of hours.

There is also a second time scheme. One human family lives through eons of time with the same problems and the same hopes while making infinitesimal progress in the evolution of the human heart.

In Harold Pinter's *Betrayal* time moves backwards as the past explains the present. Tom Stoppard's *Arcadia* has scenes from present and past in the same setting, as the present tries to explain the past—and gets it mostly wrong. The play ends with characters from both periods on stage at the same time—tough to follow in a movie but easy in a play.

In the theatre, one way or another, the gridwork of human and natural processes keeps time moving and establishes the base note, the pulse of life of every play. And yet, you may still feel that a play is not "going somewhere," which is to say, you don't feel that *you* are going somewhere—i.e., making a purposeful journey to a destination. That's the function of the structure.

We have now arrived at the hard part. Designing a structure that keeps the audience moving purposefully through time can be torture for any playwright. It's also not easy to take apart and describe. As in any dissection, first we kill the specimen and then we try to figure out what made it alive.

Let's start with a basic strand of moving architecture that's simple and powerful. A primary structural element of every play is an event that looks like it's going in one direction, then turns around and goes in another direction. This is basic to a play, an act, a scene, a sequence, or a line, especially a line of comedy.

In the first act of Garson Kanin's *Born Yesterday*, Harry Brock, a crooked businessman who always gets his way, wants to hire Paul Verrall, an honest reporter, to shape up Billie Dawn, his ex-chorus-girl mistress, and make her socially acceptable to the Washington officials he's bribing. Brock believes anybody can be bought. His lawyer, a once-honest man who knows the reporter, says Paul is not for sale. Brock begins with a deceptive casualness, describing Billie as "a good kid. Only to tell you the truth, a little on the stupid side." In his crude ignorant manner, he explains that Billie was smart enough to be a chorus girl, but she's never been around the kind of people she'll meet now. He wants Paul to smarten her up so she won't embarrass him. As you expect, Paul turns him down. Then Brock offers Paul two hundred dollars a week.

This little sequence has been designed to make you expect a cutting retort from the honest reporter to the crook. Instead he says: "All right, I'll do it."

The stage direction remarks that everyone is surprised, including the reporter. Including you, the audience, which is why you laugh. (Actually you laugh a lot more when the joke isn't being dissected.) The design makes the scene look like it's going one way, then it moves sharply in another. Not only does the scene move, you move with it. (Note: If the characters realize they're in a design, they will go dead. If there's no design, the audience will go dead. The proper handling of the tension between audience, characters, and design is where the art is).

In your privileged seat you leaned forward with anticipation, expecting an outcome that would make you feel smarter than the loud-mouthed crook who thinks he's the only smart guy in the room. When the scene turns around, you realize you've been fooled. The crook was right. He knows more than you thought.

Then comes the after-taste in the form of questions: Is everyone for sale? Or is there a good story here for the reporter? Or is it the girl he's interested in?

Are you ahead of everyone on the stage or behind everyone on the stage? Sometimes you're the one and sometimes you're the other. In either case, the playwright is keeping you moving. It's like a football play, in which

on how it's played and the reactions of
or takes her comment as an accusation
elf-pitying irony: "Everyone's kept up,
blissfully happy."

idity from the old woman who (unlike
e you) has no idea what's going on,
f place. Having pushed the scene (and
playwright now finishes off a little mir-

rebryakov, tenderly) What is it, my dear?
a pain myself in my legs that keeps
e that. (Arranges his lap robe.) It's that
Vera Petrovna, Sonya's mother, used to
just killing herself...She loved you so
, like little ones, want somebody to feel
body feels sorry for the old. (Kisses
ulder.) Come, my dear, go to bed
ey...I'll give you some linden tea, and
a prayer for you...
Let us go, Marina...

e who's moved by this unexpected turn
leads him out. Of all the people in the
to take care of old cranky babies. You
ed by the old leading the old.

aceted jewel, revealing this or that sur-
just the words, it's the way a sequence

---

a runner lowers a shoulder to make the defensive back anticipate a turn and commit himself. Then the runner surprises the defensive back by going the other way. If the defensive back stays cool and refuses to commit himself, he will not be fooled and he'll nail the runner.

The playwright does not want you sitting back and calmly judging. He needs you to be moving in a direction, vigorously anticipating. Only then can he surprise you, sometimes with comedy, sometimes with shock, sometimes with fear or hope, and occasionally with insight.

No movement, no anticipation. No anticipation, no surprise. No surprise, no delight.

One other thing to notice about this sequence: The honest reporter is being tested. Harry Brock is being tested. The lawyer is being tested. Almost every scene of a good play contains a test of character, with you anticipating the outcome and then being surprised at what actually happens.

Chekhov has the audience moving with almost every sequence of a few lines. In the opening scene of *The Seagull*, Konstantin, a young writer, stamps out in fury when his mother, Arkadina, the famous actress, pokes fun at his attempt to present his new kind of drama on a makeshift stage by the side of a lake under moonlight. But first he makes cutting remarks to her and her lover, Trigorin, the famous novelist:

> Enough! Curtain! Bring down the curtain! *(Stamping his foot)* Curtain! (*The curtain falls.*) You must forgive me. I overlooked the fact that only the chosen few can write plays and act in them. I have infringed on a monopoly!

Konstantin is still upset when he returns a few minutes later. Everyone

97

is gone except Dorn, a doctor, who tells Konstantin he liked the play. You anticipate another cutting remark from a prickly frustrated artist. What you get is a young man so happy to get praise from anyone that he embraces the doctor and almost weeps: "So you're telling me—to keep at it?"

You smile. That's the first surprise. Now the doctor starts talking about the artist's life:

> ...If it had ever been my lot to experience the exaltation that comes to artists in their moments of creation, I believe I should have despised this material shell of mine and all that pertains to it, and I'd have soared to the heights, leaving earthy things behind me.

And how does the young artist answer? He says, "Excuse me, where is Nina?"

You smile again—another surprise. You anticipated that once Konstantin had a sympathetic ear, he'd talk more about his play, but like all writers Konstantin does not want discussion, he wants praise. As soon as he's got it, he's finished with art and is off on something else—his love life, or lack of it. What's really bothering him is that a girl he is not interested in has been chasing him, while Nina, the young girl who performed in his play, has run off. You understand that the play was done as much to impress Nina as to show off his ideas about the new drama to his mother.

It's not a laugh; it's a sudden illumination of character that makes you smile because again it's caught you leaning in the wrong direction. Konstantin's frustrations as failed artist and failed lover are tangled together. This is revealed to you in a few lines as you are drawn through

for a chuckle, maybe, depen
the exhausted people. The p
and he replies with exaspera
everyone's worn out, I alone

You're anticipating one more
you) notices nothing and (
except that the samovar is o
you) firmly in one direction,
acle of construction.

> **MARINA:** (*Going up*
> Does it hurt? I've
> droning and dronin
> old complaint of you
> be up nights with y
> much...(*Pause*) Old f
> sorry for them, but
> Serebryakov on the
> now...Come along, c
> warm your feet...I'll s
> **SEREBRYAKOV:** (*Move*

The professor is not the only
as the old nurse gets him up a
household, only she knows he
are surprised, pleased, and tou

A Chekhov play is like a man
face as the light strikes it. It's r

has been set up to get you committed to thinking one way, then turning you in another direction to find something unexpected, all the more unexpected because you—in your privileged seat—had anticipated something else. You are not just watching a play. You are in movement, you are making discoveries, you are playing your part.

What's true for a brief sequence is true for a whole scene. In act one, scene four of *Romeo and Juliet*, Romeo Montague and his friends swagger in uninvited to the Capulets' ball (threatened moment). We've already seen hot-tempered Montagues and Capulets—committed enemies—fighting in the street over a trifle. Romeo is in a desperate mood over the loss of a girlfriend. You fear he's heading for trouble.

Then Romeo Montague looks at Juliet Capulet and asks a servant who she is. At the same moment, Tybalt, Juliet's fiery cousin, recognizes Romeo. He wants to attack him. It could end up in a duel or a brawl, but it doesn't. Old Capulet insists Romeo be treated as a guest. The scene, which has been making you anticipate another fight, now turns around as Romeo and Juliet approach each other (stolen moment). It's love at first sight, and a new commitment is sealed with a kiss.

This is not just an ordinary scene that appears to be moving in one direction and then turns in another. This is a key scene. Everything that happens now will flow from the kiss of commitment between two enemies. Every moment will be more precious to you—with more hope, more fear, more anticipation, more urgency—as the commitment to love in the small story will test out the commitment to hate in the large story of the feuding families. You're now in the middle of the play. The world of feeling is clashing with the world of tradition. You know which side you're on. You know what you want. You've made your own commitment. You have moved from fear for Romeo to a rush of hope for two kids in love. The play—and your role—are "going somewhere."

The key scene in Chekhov's *The Seagull* is also sealed with a kiss. This is one of those plays that has visual design as well as movement through time. Looked at in pictorial terms, *The Seagull* is a four-sided play. A famous actress, Arkadina, and her lover, the famous novelist Trigorin, have come to spend a few weeks on her country estate. Meanwhile, Arkadina's son, Konstantin, a would-be writer who lives on the estate, is in love with a local girl, Nina, a would-be actress. When Nina meets Trigorin, there is something unsaid between them (which only you notice). The design of the play deals with the effect of this interaction on the four-sided shape.

Konstantin is jealous of Trigorin, as a successful writer, and maybe as his mother's lover, and maybe for his growing interest in Nina. Arkadina may be jealous of her son's youth. She puts down his artistic pretensions as he puts down her commercial success. Nina dreams of a life of fame and happiness in the theatre. You're not sure how she feels about Konstantin. It is obvious she's infatuated with Trigorin. He is interested in Nina because he knows nothing about young girls and their psychology. He's thinking about another story.

The relationships in *The Seagull* are complicated; the basic engine of the play is simple. The key scene (end of act three) occurs when Trigorin and Arkadina are about to return to Moscow. Nina comes to say good-bye. It looks as though she and Trigorin will never see each other again (urgency). You expect a sad farewell between the provincial girl and the sophisticated artist. Then, suddenly, Nina tells Trigorin she has decided she will go to Moscow to become an actress. He kisses her, and that kiss seals something between them—an unspoken commitment.

Everyone will be affected by the kiss as the new commitment tests the old commitments of all four characters. Arkadina and Konstantin, the rejected mother and son, will turn on each other. Nina—innocent, vulnerable—will try to live her noble illusions about the theatre. You—the realist—desperately want Nina to be happy. You also fear for her as you anticipate her future with Trigorin, the detached writer, who uses people for material, not love. The play is "going somewhere," and so are you. Your role is changing—from being the good detective and anticipating the future—to hoping desperately that Nina will be successful in her new world and at the same time desperately fearing what this new world will do to her. The outer story of her commitment to the theatre will be tested out by the inner story of her love for a cool and selfish writer.

Let's look at one more key scene that ends with a kiss and a change in your role. Paul Verrall, the reporter in *Born Yesterday*, has been hired by Harry Brock to educate his mistress, Billie Dawn. In the last sequence of act one, Paul appears with newspapers and books for Billie to read. She's not interested. He persists. She gets annoyed. "Look, if you're gonna turn out to be a pest, we could call the whole thing off right now." It looks like the experiment to educate her will stop before it even starts. Then, suddenly, the scene turns and they are kissing.

It's not completely unexpected. She had made a suggestion about sex in a previous scene, and he had appeared to consider it. What does this kiss mean? Is Billie offering Paul one night of bliss? Or is there something more here? They really do like each other. A commitment may be forming that will test out the inner story of her commitment to Harry, as well as the outer story of his attempt to bribe his way into a big deal.

You are also making a commitment. You're choosing sides. You'd rather see Billie with Paul than with Harry. But you can also see threats ahead for a woman who is brash and crass on the outside, innocent and vulnerable within.

A key scene does not always involve a kiss, but it's always marked by a new commitment that will test out other commitments in both the inner and outer story. And it's usually marked by a change in your role. Your hopes and fears intensify. You choose sides. You know what you want.

Sometimes a single scene is not sufficient to complete a movement that starts you in one direction and then turns you sharply in another. Sometimes it takes a sequence of scenes, as in Shakespeare's *Measure for Measure* where the Duke of Vienna has left the city and put his deputy, Angelo, a cold-hearted Puritan, in charge of enforcing the laws. Angelo arrests a young man, Claudio, by invoking an unused law against unmarried sex. Claudio's crime: making pregnant the woman he is soon to marry. The penalty: having his head cut off three days hence. Meanwhile, Claudio's sister, Isabella, who is a novice in a nunnery, goes to Angelo to plead for her brother's life.

Act two, scene two: Claudio is to be executed in the morning (urgency). Isabella comes to Angelo with Claudio's friend Lucio and formally asks for mercy. With an officer at his side, Angelo coldly refuses. Lucio prompts Isabella to beg for mercy. She turns eloquent, pleading with Angelo to be gentle with his absolute authority:

> O, it is excellent
> To have a giant's strength, but it is tyrannous
> To use it like a giant.

Lucio is moved. The officer is moved. Angelo only says he'll think about it. Isabella leaves, offering to pray for Angelo. Roughly the way you anticipated the scene would go. Your role: You hear the promptings from Lucio that Angelo does not hear, and hope that he may be persuaded. Then the scene takes a fantastic turn.

In an aside that only you hear, Angelo reveals that the virtuous Isabella excites him. He wants to see her again because he lusts after her. Wow! What a turn! He can't believe his own feelings. And, of course, only you in your privileged seat know what's happening.

Isabella meets with Angelo once more. He offers her a deal—her brother's life for a night with him. She turns him down, she'd rather die.

What if Shakespeare eliminated the first scene and went right into the second with Angelo's offer? What's lost? First, your anticipation followed by your surprise. Second, the deep irony that Isabella's angelic plea is sexual turn on for the Puritan. Third, Angelo's struggle with himself. Fourth, believability. It takes time for this sort of thing to happen—it needs the spark and the agony, then the plan. But this is just the beginning of the sequence.

Act three, scene one: Claudio's cell. The Duke appears disguised as a monk and gives Claudio some philosophical consolation, telling the condemned man that death is a release from all the pains of life. Claudio agrees. He's ready to die. Not a brilliant scene, actually the sentiments are rather conventional.

All right, you say to yourself, this is what these people (and presumably the author) believe. You may have walked into the theatre believing some of this yourself. Whatever your beliefs, this exchange, which you will remember, becomes the key to your role in the rest of the sequence.

Isabella arrives and tells Claudio there's no hope for him. He says: "If I must die, / I will encounter darkness as a bride, / And hug it in mine arms." Same ideas you just heard, expressed poetically (actually the poetry here is pretty ordinary). The scene is going the way you anticipated, with the religious girl and the noble brother. You fear for his life and you're touched by his steadfastness.

Then Isabella reveals what Angelo offered her: "If I would yield him my virginity, / Thou might'st be freed."

Claudio comes up with the response you expect, expressed again in pretty ordinary words: "O heavens, it cannot be!"

Isabella says this very night is the time that she would have to do what she cannot even name. Bravely, Claudio says: "Thou shalt not do't."

Nobly, Isabella replies: "Oh, were it but my life, / I'd throw it down for your deliverance / As frankly as a pin."

He thanks her. She tells him to be ready for death. Probably they embrace—a noble brother, a noble sister. What's your role at the moment? Not too much. Just congratulating two noble people on their nobleness. If the scene is a test for Claudio, he's passing his test very well. Then he goes on, almost to himself:

> Yes. Has he affection in him
> That thus can make him bite the law by th' nose
> When he would force it?

What does that mean? You're puzzled for a moment. Then Claudio continues, almost out of nowhere: "Sure it is no sin, / Or of the deadly seven it is the least."

Suddenly you're laughing. What kind of turn has this scene taken? After all the noble talk, and just when you're congratulating two noble people—is Claudio suggesting what you think he's suggesting?

Isabella is slower than you to understand what's happening. Of course, the actress can play Isabella smart, in which case you lose your role and there's no laugh. Let's hope she plays it a little thickheaded, so you can be amused at her slow realization of what you saw instantly:

> ISABELLA: Which is the least?
> CLAUDIO: If it were damnable, he being so wise,
> Why would he for the momentary trick
> Be perdurable fined? O Isabel!
> ISABELLA: What says my brother?

Now Claudio continues with some of the greatest lines of Shakespeare, no longer a desperate sophist but a terrified condemned man:

> Ay, but to die, and go we know not where;
> To lie in cold obstruction, and to rot;
> This sensible warm motion to become
> A kneaded clod, and the dilated spirit
> To bathe in fiery floods, or to reside
> In thrilling region of thick-ribbed ice;
> To be imprisoned in the viewless winds,
> And blown with restless violence round about
> The pendent world; or to be worse than worst
> Of those that lawless and incertain thought
> Imagine howling—'tis too horrible!
> The weariest and most loathed worldly life
> That age, ache, penury, and imprisonment

Can lay on nature is a paradise
To what we fear of death.

He concludes by saying: "Sweet sister, let me live."

What a turn for Claudio and Isabella! And what a turn for you. You ran full tilt into a wall of brilliantly expressed reality that sent you spinning, flipping you and your illusions upside-down. As the scene moves from cardboard nobility to emotional honesty, you're surprised, amused, then startled, and perhaps even stunned by Claudio's fierceness. The amazing thing is, when you heard the truth you knew it instantly.

How did you get so smart?

Everything in this sequence of scenes is designed to prepare your reaction to Claudio's speech. You don't have a lot of time to think in the theatre. You can't stop the play to puzzle over a line. You have to make quick judgments. How do you know something? You measure it against something else. Here, the playwright is guiding you with strong clear contrasts. The earlier scenes that showed you conventional attitudes toward sex and death are there to give you a baseline of pieties—theirs, and perhaps even yours. When these conventional attitudes are ripped off, you recognize bedrock feelings. Put another way: having first heard the phony, you can't miss the real thing.

Important question: Why not have Claudio express his real feelings without the conventional scenes coming first? Wouldn't we recognize truth whenever we heard it? Forget for a moment the loss of your movement (from anticipation to surprise) and think about psychology. We all know that when people are under stress the first things they say are not always the truth. Life is filled with concealments.

Remember Parritt, the guilt-ridden boy in O'Neill's *The Iceman Cometh*? In act two he confesses to turning over his anarchist friends to the police because it was his patriotic duty. Although his mother was one of them, he was shocked when she got caught. He never wanted that to happen. Do we believe him? Maybe. In act three he says he did it for money so he could have a good time with a whore, and he absolutely did not want his mother caught, despite the fact that she controlled his life and he has no idea which of her many lovers is his father. Now do we believe him? Well...In act four he says he turned his mother over to the police because he hated her. That we believe.

In theatre as in life, illusion comes first, then reality. The design of these scenes in *Measure for Measure* gets you to commit to the one, then sharply turns you around to face the other. You are on a journey, not just from anticipation to surprise, but from illusion to reality.

After Claudio says, "Sweet sister, let me live," you pray that Isabella will fall weeping into his arms. She doesn't. Death has tested his principles and revealed his imperfect humanity. Now it's her turn.

"O, you beast!" she says. "O, faithless coward, O dishonest wretch." She tells him to die quickly, and walks out, hurtling the play forward, and you with it. But you—in your privileged seat—have an advantage over the despondent Claudio and his outraged sister that keeps you in your distinct role. You know that the Duke is watching over the action and you hope in the end he will set things right.

There are some plays that lead you in one direction for an entire act, then in the next act turn you violently around, forcing you to rethink everything you thought you knew. David Mamet's controversial 1992 play, *Oleanna*, opens in a university office with a professor and a student facing each other across a desk. The student is having problems in class. Everyone seems to understand what's going on except her. She can't go home a failure. She has to pass. Her whole future, everything she worked for, is threatened. She needs help. "Teach me," she pleads.

The professor is rushed, distracted by phone calls from his wife. There are problems with the house they're buying. He has to leave—a pressing appointment. The student flails around in despair. "I don't *understand.* I don't understand what anything means...and I walk around. From morning 'til night: with this one thought in my head. I'm *stupid.*"

This cry from the heart, familiar to everyone who's been a college freshman, touches the professor. He asks her to sit down. He knows how she feels. There was a time when he too felt like a stupid kid who deserved to fail. For a moment they seem to understand each other. Another phone call from his wife gets him frazzled. More urgent house problems. He should leave—but he doesn't. The student wonders why the professor stays to talk to her. "Because I like you," he says.

Earlier he spoke humorously of her "obeisance" in coming to see him. Now he tries to avoid appearing as the all-knowing, all-powerful professor. He suggests they drop notions of teacher and student. He apologizes when he interrupts her or uses words unfamiliar to her. To gain her trust, he confesses that he too has problems—his wife, his work, his disgust with the stupid committee that's granting him tenure.

He tries to remove the pressure of a bad grade. She hasn't failed; he's failed. She can forget about the exam. She will get an "A"—if she will come back and meet with him. They'll start the course all over again, just the two of them.

But there are rules, she says. We'll break them, he answers. She doesn't understand why he would do this. "I like you," he repeats. They'll study together. "There's no one here but you and me."

He starts a dialogue with her about education. She takes notes so she'll get everything right. He wants her to put her notebook away. He wants her to question, to challenge, to think.

He tells her a provocative story about someone at the university who once told him that the rich copulate less often than the poor, but when they do they take off more of their clothes. That stupid idea became an article of faith for him until he learned to think. The point is that no idea—neither the trivial nor the serious—is sacred at the university. Everything can be examined, even questions like: Should every kid go to college? And is higher education nothing more than "hazing" or "ritualized annoyance"?

The student doesn't understand what he's talking about. She's a lower class girl who has struggled to get this far. All she wants is to learn something and have a little success in the world. The more the professor talks, the more confused she is. Any time she comes close to understanding anything, the phone interrupts.

She falls into a panic. He puts his arm around her. "NO," she says and backs away. He tries to comfort her. She wants to reveal something to him. He urges her on. "That's all right. Tell me." The phone rings.

You are thirty minutes into the play. You should be in your privileged perch, questioning, evaluating, and anticipating what's going to happen next. But—and this is very strange—you seem to have been given no special knowledge to put you in your role. Where is the crucial information that only you hear? The gesture that only you notice? The threat that only you are aware of? The answer is: nowhere. The play is perfectly clear and perfectly opaque.

Do you have a privileged seat at *Oleanna*? Is there anything you know that they don't?

Well, you may notice that the setting—desk and chairs on a raised platform against a black background—reminds you of a boxing ring as much as a professor's office. But that doesn't tell you a lot at the moment.

And, of course, you—and only you—know the title of the play: *Oleanna*. What does that tell you? You have no idea what Oleanna means, but it must mean something. Its very mysteriousness urges you on. You push into the play. The play pushes back.

There is one possible clue. Like the audience in *Oedipus*, you bring some knowledge with you to *Oleanna*. Let's go back to the beginning. When the curtain rises, you see a female college student alone in the office of a male professor.

I've taught in colleges. If a female student walks into my office, I leave the door open. You know why. We've all read those newspaper stories. Professor condemned for inappropriate comments. Professor suspended for unwanted advances. "He made me sleep with him in exchange for higher grades." Professor sues university for false accusations.

As soon as you see a male professor alone with a female student, you automatically look for clues. But you don't find any. Everything's out in the open, and it's all moving in one direction. The girl is innocent and vulnerable. She may seem neurotic, even a bit strange, but you care about her. The only question is: Can she be helped by the distracted professor? That's the outer story. You see no inner story. And yet, there remains the nagging feeling that something more is here. This sense of withholding keeps you leaning forward in your seat. Like the student, you're desperate to understand. The playwright gives nothing away. He makes you come back for the next act.

Act two begins with the same stage picture: professor and student facing each other across the desk. The professor is talking. There is something different about him. You're not sure what it is.

He's explaining himself—his love of teaching, and the importance of getting tenure. Although he speaks in his convoluted professorial manner, you notice his tone has changed. The sense of easy authority is gone. In act one, no matter how deferential his words, he was still a tenured (almost) professor in charge of a very young student. Now, as he talks about the coming Tenure Committee meeting, there is a note of anxiety in his voice. Anxiety about what?

Then the words: "…and hear your complaint…" You realize that something has happened. You were with the action, now you're behind. You concentrate, trying to catch up.

The student has also changed. You notice that as the professor has grown more tentative, the student has become more forceful. Her confusion, her desperation—all gone. Now she's focused, even aggressive. When he uses a word she doesn't know, she tells him sharply to use another one.

He apologizes to her for being pedantic. He sees he's angered her. He understands. He too was angry with his teachers. He speaks carefully of his "unflinching concern" for his students' dignity. Every student has the right to complain. But by the time her complaint is heard and dismissed, the professor and his family will have lost their new house and the down payment. He has asked her to come today to see if they can work out the problem without the hearing. "What have I done to you?" he asks. "And…how can I make amends?"

She accuses him of trying to "force" her to retract her accusations. That's not what he meant. He's just trying to understand what has happened. He reads from her report to the Tenure Committee, which accuses him of being sexist, elitist, "wasting time in nonproscribed, self-aggrandizing and theatrical diversions from the prescribed text that have taken sexist and pornographic forms…Told a rambling sexually explicit story in which the frequency and attitudes of fornication of the poor and rich are, it would seem, the central point…moved to *embrace* said student…He said he 'liked' me. That he 'liked being with me.' He'd let me write my examination paper over if I could come back often to see him in his office…He told me he had problems with his wife and that he wanted to take off the artificial stricture of Teacher and Student. He put his arm around me…"

Is this the same bewildered student who felt her life would be over if she failed a course? You thought she was the innocent and vulnerable one. Now it's the professor's turn. Everything in his life that appeared secure—his house, his job, his future—is getting shaky. Suddenly he seems very fragile.

And you? The audience. You are in furious movement, first trying to catch up and then to make sense out of what you're hearing. Everything you thought you understood in the first act has been challenged. Before there were no clues. Now there are clues everywhere.

Yes, that was an odd story to tell a student. And why did he get so personal? "There's no one here but you and me"—why did he say that? And why did he put his arm around her? Was he using his authority to seduce a powerless student? Or is he a naïve professor being ambushed by a convert to a radical group?

As I said earlier, the audience at *Oleanna* brings knowledge with it to the theatre. But unlike the ancient Greek audience at *Oedipus*, there's no general agreement about how that knowledge is to be interpreted.

The politically correct student may cheer the girl on and feel the professor is getting what he deserves; the conservative may be appalled at the girl and demand the professor wake up and fight back. The middle-of-the-road audience may not yet know what to think.

One thing the entire audience will agree on. This is the key scene. A commitment has been made that will test everything that has gone before, and everything that happens now will flow from this moment. An inner story (however it's interpreted) has appeared, bringing with it urgency and heightened hopes and fears.

Your role is changing. You are deciding what you believe and what you want to see happen. You are making choices. Which side will you be on?

*   *   *

There is another kind of scene that is unique to the middle of a play. It has the same architecture (moving one way, then turning in another) as a key scene. But it is more central to the structure. It is the turn-around scene.

By the end of act two of *Romeo and Juliet*, the two kids have met and fallen in love. Friar Laurence marries them and hopes their feuding families can be reconciled:

> For this alliance may so happy prove
> to turn your households' rancour to pure love.

This notion gets tested in the first scene of act three, which begins with a street quarrel between Tybalt, a Capulet cousin of Juliet, and Romeo's friend, Mercutio. Romeo appears and tries to calm them, pleading with Tybalt that he has news that will make them friends. Tybalt taunts Romeo who refuses to take offense. Mercutio, angry with Romeo, challenges Tybalt.

"Gentle Mercutio, put thy rapier up," says Romeo to his friend, acting on his new belief that love can heal old quarrels. But the reality of inbred hatred is too strong. Tybalt and Mercutio fight, and Romeo, drawing his sword to stop them, inadvertently causes the death of Mercutio.

Suddenly, Romeo is being tested and your role has changed. You're no longer the good detective, analyzing, then anticipating Romeo's actions. You are committed to his happiness. You have hopes and fears for him. The question now is: What do you want Romeo to do? You want him to remember his love for Juliet. You want to shout down at him: "Get out of there!"

But his friend is dead and his honor is at stake. He's still a Montague facing a Capulet. He kills Tybalt. The scene, which began moving in one direction, has suddenly turned. You wanted peace; you're getting war.

There is more to it. Step back and look at the play as a whole. This scene (act three, scene one) represents the height of what may be called the illusion line of the play. We've talked earlier about characters living their illusions, pressing forward with their dreams, hopes, and misconceptions, to be corrected in time by reality.

In this case, Romeo is living his innocent illusion that his love for Juliet is stronger than the mindless hatred of their families. All the earlier scenes have led up to this point. Romeo has moved from one world to another. His old commitment to tradition has been replaced by his new commitment to love. The inner story is testing the outer story. There will be consequences for many.

As Romeo's sword enters the body of Tybalt, not just this scene, but the entire play pivots around and leaves the upward track of illusion and starts down the track of reality. Romeo has made his choice and he will pay the price. What looked like one kind of play has turned into another kind of play. You had hoped for a love story; you are getting a tragic story of fate.

Romeo doesn't quite see it yet. He says: "O, I am fortune's fool"—and runs. He still has hopes; you know better. And yet, even though you know his fate, some tiny fragile hope continues to live in this and every other play, to balance off threat and keep you moving in your role. Maybe Romeo will escape punishment this time. Maybe Nora's husband will take the blame for what she did. Othello may discover Iago's plot. Nina may find happiness with Trigorin.

The turn-around scene is not what is ordinarily called the climax of the play. It is sometimes a very small scene. Sometimes it's a scene that does not even appear on the stage. But there is always a huge shift of motion, as the play goes from the track of illusion to the track of reality.

The turn-around scene in *Antony and Cleopatra* (act three, scene ten) is very brief and does not include either Antony or Cleopatra. It starts with sounds of a sea battle offstage. Antony and Octavius Caesar are fighting a war for control of the Roman world. Octavius has dared Antony to fight at sea, where Octavius is strong. Despite the advice of his followers, Antony has accepted the dare, with Cleopatra promising to contribute her navy. Antony has been moving upward on the track of illusion, believing he can win the war (outer story), and keep Cleopatra's love (inner story) without having to choose between them.

In the middle of the unseen battle (urgency), Antony's friend and follower, Enobarbus, enters to announce that Cleopatra has run from the battle along with her whole fleet. He is so distraught that he has turned away, unable to watch any more. Another of Antony's followers, Scarus, enters and Enobarbus questions him:

> **ENOBARBUS:** How appears the fight?
> **SCARUS:** On our side like the tokened pestilence
> Where death is sure. Yon riband-red nag of Egypt—
> Whom leprosy o'ertake!—i'th'midst o'th'fight—
> When vantage like a pair of twins appeared,
> Both as the same, or rather ours the elder–
> The breeze upon her, like a cow in June,
> Hoists sails and flies.
> **ENOBARBUS:** That I beheld.
> Mine eyes did sicken at the sight, and could not
> Endure a further view.
> **SCARUS:** She once being luffed,
> The noble ruin of her magic, Antony,
> Claps on his sea-wing and, like a doting mallard,
> Leaving the fight in height, flies after her.
> I never saw an action of such shame.

Experience, manhood, honour, ne'er before
Did violate so itself.

The battle is lost. The Egyptian slut has run away in the middle of the fight, and Antony has run after her, abandoning his troops. At this point, the entire play turns around and leaves the track of illusion and moves on to the track of reality. The inner story of Antony's love for Cleopatra has been tested by the outer story of war. Antony has made his choice. He has moved from the hard, practical Roman world to the soft, passionate Egyptian world. Everything in the play has led up to this moment, and now everything slopes away from this moment. The consequences come quickly. Another of Antony's followers appears and announces his decision to abandon him.

> CAMIDIUS: To Caesar will I render
> My legions and my horse. Six kings already
> Show me the way of yielding.

The fated course of the play has been set. It appeared as something gloriously romantic, now it's turning into tragedy. You're no longer the good detective anticipating the future. You have a stake in the action. When Antony agreed to fight at sea, you wanted to shout down at him: "Dummy, don't do it!" And when Cleopatra ran from the battle you hoped to God he wasn't going to chase after her. "Win the battle and meet her in Alexandria, you fool!"

As the play wheels around, you move from large hopes to fragile hopes. All is not lost immediately. Antony wins a small battle, and yet it will soon be apparent that the price of love will not only be the loss of their empire, but also their lives.

Will it be worth it? You'll have the rest of the play to make your judgment, as the lovers face their fate with some of Shakespeare's most passionate poetry, which may convince you that love can conquer death. (Or you may prefer to see the lovers as two selfish superstars who care little for anyone but themselves.)

Aristotle notes in *The Poetics* that in the middle of *Oedipus the King* a messenger arrives, "coming to gladden Oedipus and to remove his fears..." The poor king can use some good news. He's searching for the killer of Laius, the previous king, whose unavenged murder has caused the plague that's killing everybody in Thebes (urgency). Oedipus has told the people they don't have to pray to the gods for help. He, Oedipus, will grant their prayers (the arrogance of his illusions of power).

He offers a reward for information about the killer and he curses anyone who has knowledge and keeps silent. He also curses the killer. He even curses himself if the killer turns out to be some one in his own family (not a good career move, considering what you—with your godlike abilities—already know.)

Then a blind prophet, Tiresias, appears and reluctantly tells Oedipus that he himself is the killer (outer story)—and he hints at worse things to be revealed about his parents and his marriage (inner story). You, of course, know Oedipus is the killer. You also know what's going to be revealed about who he is. If you've forgotten, Tiresias turns to the audience (after Oedipus walks away) and says plainly that he is brother and father to his children and son and husband to his mother.

Oedipus fights back with the illusion that Tiresias and his brother-in-law Creon are in a plot to destroy him. He wants Creon dead. Creon says there is no plot. He simply believes in the words of the gods and their prophets. Oedipus puts himself above the gods. Two worlds at war.

Jocasta, wife of Oedipus, intervenes in their fight. She will not attack the gods, but she has proof that prophets and oracles can make mistakes. An oracle said her husband King Laius would be killed by his own son, so they got rid of their son when he was a newborn, binding his ankles and having him left on a barren mountain to die. In addition, she knows from a shepherd who witnessed the murder that her husband the king was killed, not by a single man, but by a band of strangers at a place where three roads meet. The oracle got it wrong.

This should create more hope in Oedipus. Instead, it jogs his memory of something from the past. He questions Jocasta about the murder—when and where it happened. Her answers leave him shaken. He realizes he may have cursed himself. He must find the witness and question him.

The anguished Oedipus remembers his early life as the son of the King of Corinth, and the drunken man who said he was not the King's son, and the oracle that told him he would kill his father and marry his mother. He ran away from Corinth to save himself from the prophecy and later killed some men at a crossroad who attacked him. One of the men resembled Jocasta's description of her husband the king.

It doesn't look good for Oedipus. He and Jocasta desperately hang on to the shepherd's story that Laius was killed by a band of men, not just one. You watch Oedipus running from elation to despair and back again, as the play moves upward with strokes of threat followed by counterstrokes of hope. You—the audience—are moving in a different direction. You see the net tightening around Oedipus. Your fear for him grows. You lean forward with anticipation to see how he will react to the truth you already know.

The chorus (which represents the beliefs of the Athenian audience) steps in to say that it will never give up its reverence for the will of the mighty gods. A man who says he has no reverence for the gods deserves his doom. All religion will collapse unless the prophecies of the oracle come true and the absolute authority of the gods is maintained. You may not believe this yourself, but you feel its power. You know there will be no mercy for Oedipus.

Jocasta appears with a suppliant's branch and prays to Apollo to set them free from the hollow prophecies of the human servants of the gods (a nice distinction). Then, as if in answer to her prayer, the messenger enters with news for Oedipus that will "gladden his heart and remove his fears."

Wait a minute. Could there be some unforeseen way out for Oedipus? Has the playwright changed the story? Is there some hope after all? Did the Athenian audience want Oedipus to escape his fate? I doubt it. Do you? I think so. At this point, both audiences lean forward with anticipation to hear what the messenger has to say.

Full of good cheer, the messenger announces that the people of Corinth want to make Oedipus king. The old king, Oedipus' father, is dead. Oedipus is suddenly elated. He ran from Corinth because the oracle prophesied that he was fated to kill his father and marry his mother. Now he says with enormous relief:

The prophecies of the gods are worthless.

This is the top of the illusion line of the play. But the more Oedipus feels relief, the more you feel anguish. The higher he gets, the farther will be his fall. Oedipus is not completely at ease; his mother still lives.

When he expresses his fear of the other half of the prophecy, Jocasta comforts him:

> What should a man fear? It's all chance, chance rules our lives. Not a man on earth can see a day ahead, groping through the dark. Better to live at random, best we can. And as for this marriage with your mother—have no fear. Many a man before you, in his dreams, has shared his mother's bed. Take such things for shadows, nothing at all—Live, Oedipus, as if there's no tomorrow.

The messenger from Corinth gives Oedipus even more comfort. He has nothing to fear from the oracle because the King and Queen of Corinth are not his real father and mother. How does he know? It just so happens that he is the one who received the baby with the bound ankles (look at your scars, Oedipus) from a shepherd who was—listen closely—the servant of King Laius of Thebes. Uh, oh. The scene that looked like it might go in a hopeful direction has changed course. Who sees this? You do. You've known the story all the time. Still it's a shock to see it coming true.

The play has reached the turn-around point. The chain of evidence is nearly complete. All that is left to find out is who gave the baby to the shepherd. The stage direction reads: "*Jocasta turns sharply.*" She knows, and you—in your privileged seat—know she knows. With her turn, the play begins to pivot. Oedipus hasn't quite got it yet. He is still pushing on. Who is this shepherd? The chorus tells him that this is the same man who witnessed the killing of the king. A large coincidence, but you don't care. Your eyes are glued on Oedipus. Inner and outer stories are coming together. His life is collapsing. What will he do?

Pause for a little discussion (remember we're dissecting). I've already mentioned the kind of characters the audience cares about. Basically you care about the innocent and the vulnerable, those who are trapped and don't know it. This is certainly Oedipus' story. But there's one more element, which has been implied, that needs to be made clear. Every character you care about has to be tested and has to make choices. Watching the purely inevitable gets dull quickly because there's nothing for you to do. Romeo is tested and chooses to kill Tybalt. Antony is tested and chooses to leave the battle and follow Cleopatra. It's choices—anticipating them and being surprised by them—that keeps you in your role.

Oedipus may seem to have no choices. He's doomed and that's it. Actually he does have choices. He can be passive, do nothing. He can try to hang on to his illusions a little longer. He can kill himself out of shame. He can run away—maybe Sparta will take him in. Or—and this is what he does—he can march toward the truth.

Oedipus demands to hear from the shepherd himself. Jocasta tries to put him off, begging him to inquire no further into his past. He insists. He will not run from the truth. He will face it. "I must know it all," he says, "must see the truth at last." Arrogant, yes; but magnificently arrogant.

What if Sophocles had done it differently? What if the messenger had entered and said: "I have bad news for you, Oedipus. Your father, King of Corinth, is dead. Of course he wasn't your real father and the Queen isn't your real mother, and I happen to know all this because I was the one who received you from the shepherd, and I remember you had your ankles bound—Just the way you bound them together when you got rid of him, isn't that right, Jocasta?"

If the playwright did the scene this way, the play would go dead, and so would your role. There would be no movement for Oedipus. Just information and passive crumbling. Or information and yelling and screaming. No chance for him to make his own decision to uncover the horrible truth. No growing horror for Jocasta as she tries to stop him. And no way at all for you to charge forward into the scene anticipating Oedipus' reaction as he is tested out, and then being surprised and moved by his choice.

This is terrific scene construction. There seems nowhere to go and yet everyone is in movement as the play turns away from the upward slope of hope and illusion and starts down the slope of reality and fate. You lean forward knowing everything, yet still not knowing what is to come.

Harry Brock, the crude millionaire junk man in *Born Yesterday*, is in Washington wining, dining, and bribing senators to make a crooked deal. The question in the outer story is: will he get away with it?

Meanwhile, Paul Verrall, the liberal magazine writer Harry hired to smarten up his dumb blond girlfriend, Billie, is falling in love with her while giving her a quick book education.

As for Billie, she is slowly learning that there is someone else inside her besides the blond bimbo of a brutish man. This is the inner story. She is moving from the world of the selfish and dishonest (Harry, his lawyer, the crooked senator) to the world of the generous and decent (Paul and the hotel maid).

The turn-around scene occurs when Billie's commitment to Harry is challenged by her growing commitment to herself. The crucial play writing issue is how to make the two stories meet in a test. It happens late in the second act. On the advice of his lawyer, Harry (for tax purposes) has made Billie the president of his company. She has to put her signature on papers she never reads. This time, encouraged by her new learning, she refuses to sign anything until she understands what it's all about. Billie is getting the definite idea that Harry's business is illegal.

You've felt pretty smart as you've watched her develop, since you already know most of the things she's discovering about American history and culture and the meaning of words. You also know that she's getting involved with Paul while tied to Harry. You're trying to anticipate what's going to happen. But this is the middle of the play and there's more to your role. You know what you want. You're rooting for Billie not to sign the papers, and you want Harry stopped.

Everything in the play has led up to this point. The papers are in front of Billie. They must be signed now (urgency). The crooked lawyer has gone to the upstairs bedroom of the hotel suite to tell Harry that she has refused to sign. Downstairs, Billie studies the papers with the help of a dictionary. You know that Harry is a brute. You know that Billie is going to be tested. She can be tough, she's been around, and she knows how to get what she wants from a guy. Still she is basically innocent and vulnerable. You have hopes for her, and you're also scared for her.

The scene could move quickly; the playwright raises the tension by slowing it down. You want it, but he won't give it to you just yet. He'll even interrupt the scene twice with the maid entering to straighten up. The playwright has plenty of time. He has you now.

You're surprised by the way Harry comes downstairs, sleeves rolled up, smoking a cigarette, no veneer of a suit. His voice is oddly gentle and reasonable. He's patient, even kind. He doesn't ask her to sign the papers. He tries to embrace her. In a crude way, he's playing the romance card. She avoids him. He's exasperated, but not angry. You anticipated something brutal from a guy who is used to getting his way in everything. Maybe he loves her after all.

The scene is not going the way you thought. You thought he was going to come down the stairs and hit her. You lean forward, trying to figure out what he's going to do.

Finally he tells her to sign the papers. She won't. "I'm not gonna sign anything any more till I know what I'm signing." You think, "Hey, she's going to face him down. Good for Billie."

Then he slaps her (the exact point of the turn-around). Then he slaps her again. The first time is because he's mad, the second time is to show her who's boss.

Billie signs the papers. She sobs. You are disappointed. You had high hopes for her. Even when she pugnaciously calls him, "Big—*Fascist!*" (which she mispronounces), you feel she's been defeated. She retreats to her room.

And yet...and yet you feel something in her may have changed, that she may have gone from one world to another, that maybe she is ready to drop her old commitment to Harry and make a new commitment somewhere else. For a moment, your feelings are suspended. You're not sure what to think. Billie appears again and starts to walk out of the suite. Harry stops her with: "And don't be late if you don't want a bloody nose." You anticipate more humiliation. Then Billie turns to him and speaks ever so gently:

BILLIE: Would you do me a favor, Harry?

> **HARRY:** *(Mean, still not looking at her)* What?
> **BILLIE:** Drop dead?

So you were right the first time. Inner and outer stories have intersected with Billie's test. Harry thinks he's won. You know he may be on the way to losing—losing the girl and maybe the deal. You've moved back and forth several times in the scene, fearing, hoping, anticipating, rooting for Billie, being disappointed, then finding out the slap has changed her. Harry hired Paul to educate Billie; his slap is her real education. He thinks he's so smart, but you're smarter than he is. That's why Billie's line always gets such a huge laugh.

Everything in the play leads up to the point of the slap. It hovers there until this moment, where it finally turns around and starts in a new direction. It has moved from the illusion track, pivoted around, and started on the reality track. It had looked to you like a play about a brutal man getting his way; it has turned into a play about the birth of conscience in a not-so-dumb blonde. The stakes are rising—Billie's going to take some action. There will be consequences. And only you know it. You move with the play as it pivots around, but your role always remains distinct from every other role on the stage.

Notice something else: You feared that when Harry came downstairs he would hit Billie and make her sign the papers, and that's exactly what happened. And yet you were still surprised. Harry comes downstairs differently than you thought he would, raising your hopes about the outcome. Then, after he does hit her, you think she's been defeated, but it turns out she hasn't—and you're surprised again.

This is called misdirection. The playwright keeps your anticipations going, and even if you end up pretty much where you thought you would, you still have the sensation of movement through the scene.

Then the playwright surprises and delights you at the end with Billie's change and the play turns around and moves off on its fated path.

What if the playwright eliminated the zigzags of misdirection and got right to the point? Harry comes downstairs and hits her and she signs. Then she tells him to drop dead and walks out. What's lost?

Just as would have happened with *Oedipus*, the play would go dead. No movement. No raising the stakes. No time for your hopes and fears to develop. No time to savor the test and the choice, as Billie moves from one world to another and forms a new commitment to herself that conflicts with her old commitment to Harry.

At the end of the scene, Harry would probably be a lot more than just flabbergasted at her boldness. He might start to worry about what she could do to him and his business and thus steal a piece of your role.

In this sense, theatre mimics life. We live on our illusions, and it takes a lot of time and effort for reality to break through.

Now step back for a moment and consider the design of an entire play, the architecture that keeps you moving in your role. A play, taken as a whole, may be seen as an exercise in misdirection, as it moves from illusion to reality, from innocence to knowledge.

Why design a whole play this way? Why not move directly to reality? Then the play would be no play, and there would be no place for you. No privileged seat and nothing for you to know that they don't. No detective work and no analysis. No caring for the innocent and vulnerable who live by their illusions while you see reality. No raising the stakes to heighten fear and hope. No chance for you to choose sides, to become an advocate, to get invested in someone's life. No pleasure in the uncovering of truth. No slowing down the action to raise tension as the small story and the large story test each other. No pressing forward with anticipation and then being surprised when the play turns in a different direction. No way for your purposeful movement through the gridwork of time. No movement through layers of illusion that makes you know the truth when you see it. No heightened journey for you, with intensifying fears and hopes and desires for someone you care about, which is your role in the middle of the play.

You might be wondering what's the point of knowing all this. Will it help you enjoy the play? Why not just pay your money and watch it? Do you really want to know why you laugh, or why you cry or why you lean forward with total focus at this play and fall asleep at that play? The same questions can be asked about football or baseball. Is it more enjoyable to know or not to know something about a game when you go to see one? I guess the answer is you can enjoy it either way. For me, the deepest pleasure comes from the deepest knowledge.

*   *   *

We've just looked at the moving architecture of a line, a sequence, a scene, a sequence of scenes, key scenes, and turn-around scenes. Now let's look at the construction of a full act, and discuss the tactics that help you play your part in the middle of the play.

In act one of *Translations* you saw the first encounter of the outer story, as the world of the past is put under siege by the world of the future. The English army has come to make a modern map of Ireland. Starting in a remote corner of County Donegal, they are "correcting" all Irish place names by changing them to English, and thereby beginning the process of wiping out the Irish language (and culture and history). The unarmed, impractical Irish are responding with wit and apparent nonchalance. A few are retaliating against the English by killing English horses, a violent counter-strike.

Act one ends with the first encounter of the inner story. Owen, the Irish translator, introduces Lt. Yolland, the dreamy young English orthographer, to Maire, the up-and-doing young Irishwoman. No dialogue here, not even a stage direction for it, but you in your privileged seat see the potential in the look exchanged between them. You'll also note the jealousy in the face of Owen's brother Manus, the crippled son of the schoolmaster, and the longing for Manus in the face of Sarah, the Irish girl he is teaching to speak.

This pattern of relationships, and their potential for movement, has now been set up in the inner story. How the inner and outer stories develop and test each other is yet to come. In plays, what you do in one story always affects something or someone in the other story.

Your beginning role of using your unique knowledge to be the good detective is changing. You're wondering how the presence of Yolland will alter the relationship of Maire and Manus. You're wondering how the English will respond to the killing of the horses. You're thinking about which side you're on. You're ready to make commitments to the people you care about. You're not just anticipating, you're deciding what you want to see.

Act two, scene one is in the hedge-school several days later. You know that time has passed because the renaming process announced in the first act is now well along. Owen, surrounded by maps and reference books, is changing old Irish names to English and writing them down in a Name-Book while Yolland drinks potent Irish brew and tries to learn the odd Irish word. He's kind to the Irish at the school, giving Manus oranges he's received from Dublin, and thanking Doalty, the farmer-student, for cutting the grass around his tent. The Irishmen are contemptuous of the Englishman.

You understand all this, because in your privileged seat you understand both languages. Yolland notices nothing. He's in love with the romantic idea of Ireland. You're touched by his innocence and his illusions as he moons over Maire, fantasizes about learning the Irish language, and even plays with the idea of living in the Irish rural world. Owen, the Irish realist, is amused:

> **OWEN:** Live on what? Potatoes? Buttermilk?...For God's sake! The first hot summer in fifty years and you think it's Eden. Don't be such a bloody romantic. You wouldn't survive a mild winter here.
> **YOLLAND:** Do you think not? Maybe you're right.

Owen laughs at him, without bothering to tell the innocent Englishman that he can't even get Owen's Irish name right. Meanwhile, the stakes in the outer story are rising, announced first in minor, then in major ways. A little Irish girl spat at Yolland, and now Captain Lancey, the English commander, is searching for the Donnelly twins, the unseen menacing figures introduced in the first act. You see a pattern of escalating stroke and counter-stroke and wonder who's going to make the next move.

Here Owen appears as innocent and filled with illusions as Yolland. All he's doing is making sense out of some old Irish names and translating them into English. What's the harm? Neither one of them notices the threats that you see. Violence is in the air, but only you seem to notice it. Owen refuses to be moved even when accused by his own brother Manus of not facing what the British are doing.

What if they had fewer illusions? Then they would not be so vulnerable, and your role of seeing what they do not would disappear. It's your god-like understanding of the situation that makes you anticipate the future with fear for the innocents who have no fear for themselves. This is the engine that propels you through the moving structure of the middle of the play.

Owen's father, Hugh the schoolmaster, appears quoting a Latin poem. He takes a glass of the brew Yolland is drinking, realizes its potency, and remarks that Yolland should, "address [himself] to it with circumspection"—leading you to believe he'll now lay off the drink himself. Instead he downs another in one gulp. You laugh. You thought the little sequence was going in one direction, then it turns around and makes you laugh. Only a little character joke, but it points up the power of the drink, which you'll remember in the next scene.

More important for you, Hugh is an emblem of Ireland—witty, drunken, erudite, with knowledge and virtues that the modern world has no use for. This sets up a further contrast between Yolland and Owen. The English officer appreciates Hugh; the Irish son is embarrassed by him.

The threats to the old hedge-school in the first act are now turning into reality. Hugh announces that he's going to discuss with the builders of the new school his living accommodations when he takes it over. Very soon there'll be no more Irish learning. Hugh seems all too easy about it (another Irish innocent?), but as he toys with Yolland's enthusiastic though quite limited knowledge of poetry and language, you realize with a bit of surprise that he's playing a parody of himself. He knows very well what's happening; a world is crumbling and there's nothing he can do about it, except make high-flown erudite jokes about his language:

> Yes, it is a rich language, Lieutenant, full of the mythologies of fantasy and hope and self-deception—a syntax opulent with tomorrows. It is our response to mud cabins and a diet of potatoes; our only method of replying to...inevitabilities.

He ends with rueful realism: Irish may be "a linguistic contour that no longer matches the landscape of...fact."

Hugh sees the truth and can do nothing. He's the occupied country. Lt. Yolland agrees with Hugh, but he's only a small cog in the occupying army. Owen does not see, or does not want to see. He has both feet in the modern world of progress and rationality and a bit of contempt for his father who can't adjust to reality. Still, he loves the old man and he's sympathetic with his brother Manus who wants to stay and teach in the old language. Plays always offer alternative paths to help you measure the movements of characters. Manus has chosen one path, Owen another, without quite abandoning his feelings for family and country.

Owen's placement by the playwright in the practical rational English world is key to the basic structure of the play, because when and if he begins to move from one world to another, you will understand it instantly without having to reflect on exactly where he's been and where he's going.

You have seen the contrast between Owen and his brother Manus. Now you see the contrast between Lt. Yolland and Owen, and you appreciate the irony of the Englishman who wants to be Irish and the Irishman so at home with the English. You wonder who will move from where to where and what the consequences will be. You're anticipating something neither sees—violence—and you wonder which one is going to get hurt.

Yolland and Owen fight over one of the Irish place names they are changing—*Tobair Vree*. Yolland feels guilty because he's involved in destroying something precious. Owen goes through the whole muddled linguistic history of *Tobair Vree* that makes no sense anymore and that no one but he remembers. Yolland insists it's important that someone does remember. Owen replies with a key line: "I've left here."

While Yolland the Englishman defends the mythic Irish world about which he knows nothing, Owen the Irishman has contempt for the backward Irish world he loves but no longer inhabits. They are drinking and they are getting exasperated with each other. You wonder how far the argument will go. Once more Yolland gets Owen's name wrong and Owen explodes. Is this the spark that ignites the violence?

No, the scene flips around, and this becomes the spark that makes them both explode with laughter at the absurdity of the situation. You are surprised because you were leaning in one direction and then the scene turned you around in another. Yolland and Owen have been tested. They are friends. They pour more drinks.

Drinking scenes on the stage are common. It's another way of establishing the innocence and vulnerability of the characters and preserving your role. They're drunk and they don't realize it. You do. You smile at their exaggerations, or if they speak sincerely, you don't back away emotionally as you normally would with stage sincerity.

Manus enters to announce he's getting a school post with a real salary to teach in Irish on an island off the coast. Owen is delighted. It's not his path, but he's pleased for his brother. (You think: perhaps there is yet hope for the language.) In his happiness, Manus allows himself to become reconciled with Owen. He even speaks English to Yolland, who congratulates him on his new future. They shake hands. They all drink together. What looked like growing animosity now suddenly turns to friendship.

Three men—separated by language, history, and military occupation— with the help of a little potent alcohol can still like each other as men. For a moment, brothers reconcile, English and Irish reconcile. You are beginning to hope that the natural goodness in men's hearts can somehow bridge the artificial gulfs that separate them. Hope matters in plays, especially tragic plays. You must always feel there's a path up as well as a path down. This puts you in movement, enticing you one way and then another, making you anticipate an outcome, then surprising you with what actually happens.

Maire enters. She's not impressed with Manus' news. She's more interested in the dance tomorrow night at *Tobair Vree*. "*Tobair Vree!*" shouts the drunken Yolland. Irish words he knows! Of course he has no idea what Maire is talking about. You smile because you do.

Maire tells Owen to tell Yolland about the dance. In the middle of a play every scene is a test, and in this scene Maire has a choice of two men and she chooses the Englishman. You quickly measure her interest in Yolland by what she is giving up in Manus. (To get something in a play, you almost always have to give up something.) You may also notice the irony of Maire's interest in a man who's in love with the Irish world she wants to escape.

Despite their differences, you have hopes for Maire and Yolland. At the same time you sense a threat that they don't. Manus has left the stage and so he hasn't seen Maire's approach to Yolland. You wonder what will happen to the newfound good feelings between him and Yolland if he learns about the flirtation. You guess that if some Irishmen believe that their women are being taken, they will have one more reason for violent reaction to the English troops.

Act two, scene two is at night outside the hedge-school. It is played in darkness in front of the schoolroom set. Your imagination, helped by the Irish country music in the background, creates the scene. Yolland and Maire appear, laughing and running hand-in-hand, both talking about the leap over the ditch, the wet grass, being out of breath, and the fear (mixed with pleasure) of being missed. It's almost as though they understand each other. They don't. They're just excited by the same thing—running from the dance to be alone in the darkness. You find all this delicious because only you—in your privileged seat—understand them both.

Now, suddenly embarrassed, they separate and fall silent. They want to tell each other how they feel, but they don't know how to begin. I'm going to take apart the wonderful scene that follows and dissect it, which will kill its emotional impact (go see the play for the real thing). I want you to understand what the playwright is up to, and what his tactics are as he creates a love scene with roles for three participants—the two lovers and you.

All well-constructed love scenes are stolen moments, people where they shouldn't be, doing what they shouldn't be doing, and threatened by discovery. This gives you a way to measure the lovers' passion by letting you see what they are willing to risk to be together. Romeo Montague comes to Juliet Capulet despite their feuding families. Antony stays with Cleopatra while enemy troops attack and his followers abandon him.

Billie Dawn kisses Paul Verrall in the hotel suite of her brutish boyfriend Harry Brock. Nina has only a few moments with Trigorin before his mistress Arkadina will take him away forever. Maire, the Irish farm girl, is alone in the dark with George Yolland, the English officer, even as tensions are rising between the Irish farmers and the English troops. They know that someone will notice that they are missing from the dance, but the excitement of being together is stronger than any fear.

Lovers live their illusions; you see reality. You know they don't have much time in which to find a way to express their feelings (urgency). You begin to worry for the young lovers who don't worry enough for themselves. That puts you on the edge of your seat with hopes and fears.

A love scene without hopes and fears quickly loses altitude. It's like observing a couple smooching at the next table in a restaurant—you're happy for them, but you'd just as soon they do it someplace else. For you, as for the lovers on the stage, it's stolen pleasure that makes the moments precious.

Crucial question: How does that pleasure express itself? What actually happens in a love scene on the stage? The movies show you everything. Well, almost everything. Are Julie Christie and Donald Sutherland really doing what you think they're doing in that Venice hotel room in Nicolas Roeg's 1973 film, *Don't Look Now?* Sitting in the dark at the movie house watching naked people making love can be (it's okay to admit it) very exciting.

Theatre is different. If you watched two real people tear off their clothes and start making love right in front of you, I guarantee you would become very nervous very quickly. Being so close to someone else's passion is threatening. Ask psychologists for reasons. The important point is that in-your-face sex would make you back out of the scene, giggling nervously as you go, and that would kill your role.

The difference between lovemaking on stage and lovemaking on screen is that the screen acts as a kind of—well—screen, taking you one step away from reality and allowing you to watch even graphic sex without anxiety overload. All playwrights know instinctively that the stage must filter out some of the heat of physical passion. It's the equivalent of those dark glasses you need when you look directly into the sun.

Love on the stage is almost always rendered obliquely. Think of all the romantic plays you've ever seen. You never actually see the love scene. You see the scene before or the scene after. In the scene before—the one leading up to the scene you never see—the playwright works hard to keep the lovers apart, mainly by introducing obstacles to lovemaking. Sometimes geography frustrates them. Sometimes it's one character's reticence. Sometimes it's fear of consequences. "My wife/lover/mother/God, will kill me."

There are some exceptions: The first part of Harvey Fierstein's *Torch Song Trilogy* has some pretty explicit homosexual couplings without obstacles. If you think about it, you realize that what you're watching has more to do with loneliness than love. Pure physical passion between two people with no obstacles between them is interesting for about ten seconds. Plays with love stories are basically about getting there, not being there.

Shakespeare has no physical love scenes. *Romeo and Juliet* is his great love play, but there is only one scene that's even close to a physical scene, and that's a brief moment after they've made love, which is surrounded by threats. Romeo has to leave or he'll be killed, and Juliet's mother is about to appear to tell her she has to marry somebody else. Every other scene in *Romeo and Juliet* features the obstacles that keep them apart.

Take the famous balcony scene: the balcony itself is the obstacle. She's up there; he's down here. No way to get together. Keeping the lovers apart is what keeps you in your role. You're not just watching. You're in movement, hoping, fearing, anticipating, urging on, feeling frustrated and elated by turns. There's room for your imagination (which is more powerful than any reality) to fill the gap between what you see and what you'd like to see. The scene blossoms, not on the stage, but in your head.

Shakespeare adds another element to cool things down; he writes the scene in poetry. The formal verse acts as a screen filtering the youthful passions and keeping them from becoming too frontal. Even this is not enough. The playwright knows that seeing two ardent young lovers on the stage can still raise anxieties, so he adds something to drain off the excess emotions that could spill into inadvertent laughter. He gives you something else to laugh at.

Just before the balcony scene, Romeo's friend Mercutio appears in the garden making bawdy comments about sex. Then, during the scene itself, Juliet's nurse keeps calling to Juliet to come into the house. This adds to the stolen pleasure. Both the young lovers have to leave in a few moments (more urgency). But the essential purpose of having Mercutio on one side and the nurse on the other is to give you something to laugh at so you won't laugh at the lovers. Laughter in the wrong place is death to a play. Comedy around the fringes of a love scene gives you a quick measuring stick—that is the funny part, this is the serious part.

Obstacles in love scenes can take many forms. The main obstacle in act two, scene two of *Translations* is language. Language becomes the balcony of this scene, keeping Maire and Yolland apart as they try to grasp each other's feelings and intentions without being able to speak each other's language. This mutual lack of comprehension is the screen for their emotions and allows a space for you to play your part of understanding what they don't, even laughing at words that in another context might be too frontal, too hot, or just plain banal, but here turn into hilarious misperceptions and tender misinterpretations. It's as though the playwright has fitted you with night-vision glasses to watch two people in the dark groping for each other.

After the first awkward moment, Yolland points to himself: "George." After more sputtering in their own languages, accompanied by "What-what?" and "Sorry-sorry?", Maire points to herself: "Maire." More fumbling, then Yolland points to both of them: "Maire and George." She nods. Contact! Now what? Yolland can't decide. Maire says: "Say anything at all. I love the sound of your speech." A hint for you about something coming later—the understanding that goes beyond words.

Meanwhile, they search for anything that might help them communicate. Yolland tries an illusionary tactic: English can be understood if spoken loud enough and slow enough. Of course that doesn't work, though you find the attempt hilarious. Maire tries a third language. She speaks to Yolland in Latin. He takes it for Irish, then tells her to "say anything at all—I love the sound of your speech." They actually are in tune but they don't know it. Only you know it. How delicious.

They struggle on with single words from Maire's small store of English. "Water." "Fire." "Earth." Yolland becomes excited: "Of course—earth! Earth. Earth. Good Lord, Maire, your English is perfect!" You laugh again. Such big excitement over so little. Maire and Yolland don't laugh. They are in dead earnest. If they laughed, there would be no room for your laughter. Now that they think they're getting somewhere, Maire hopefully brings out her one sentence of English learned by rote as a child:

> MAIRE: George, in Norfolk we besport ourselves around the maypoll.
> YOLLAND: Good God, do you? That's where my mother comes from—Norfolk. Norwich actually. Not exactly Norwich town but a small village—

He rattles on, then stops abruptly realizing this is not communication. Maire misinterprets, thinking she must have said "something dirty." Embarrassed, she turns away. Yolland puts out his hand. She won't take it. She starts to move off. Yolland is desperate. You are desperate. Their struggles are heightening your hopes and fears, making every moment more intense.

Finally, he says the only Irish words he can think of—"*Bun na hAbhann*"—an Irish place name. Maire looks at him. She responds with another Irish place name—"*Lis na nGradh.*" They say them back and forth—"*Carraig an Phoill.*" "*Carraig na Ri.*" Irish place names magically turning into words of affection. "*Loch na nEan.*" "*Loch an Iubhair.*" (Heavy irony: these are the place names that Yolland is destroying and Maire wants to run away from.)

They hold hands. They speak words of tenderness, very much aware that the other does not understand. This allows them to say things to each other that would make them (and you) blush if they were understood.

He says, "I wish to God you could understand me," and then goes on: "I would tell you how beautiful you are, my curly headed Maire." Maire says lovingly, "Your arms are long and thin and the skin on your shoulders is very white." (Not like the burly sun-darkened arms of the Irish farm workers.) If they understood each other when they talked like this, there would be no role for you except to get acutely embarrassed. But here, safe behind the screen of language, you are a godlike presence, spanning the obstacles, understanding everything, feeling the poignancy and the preciousness of the first moments of love.

They tell each other they understand each other—"I know what you're saying," they say to each other, and they almost do. (Of course, there is that one little lapse in understanding—he wants to stay in Ireland and she wants to get out.) The playwright is teasing you, intensifying the suspense. Can they really connect? Can they do it right here, right now? You want to whisper to them, "Yes, yes, you're on the right track, keep going, keep going." Each begins using the same word without being aware of it.

> YOLLAND: I would tell you how I want to be here—to live here—always—with you—always, always.
> MAIRE: 'Always'? What is that word—'Always'?

Then a few moments later:

> MAIRE: I want to live with you—anywhere—anywhere at all—always—always.
> YOLLAND: 'Always'? What is that word—'always'?

They both use the same word—always—neither understanding what the other is saying. But you know that they actually do have an understanding, something from the heart that goes beyond language. Just as the three men in the outer story liberated by drink understood each other, so do the two lovers in the small story understand each other without the words that can keep people apart as easily as bring them together.

Your role has now become more than understanding what they don't, more than fearing someone will intrude on them, more than seeing the ironies or being amused at their fumbling. Your role is now focused on wanting something. You want them to get through the thicket of misunderstandings and misperceptions. You want them to realize they have come to some kind of understanding that goes beyond words. Face it—you want to see them kiss.

When you finally get what you want, and the English lieutenant kisses the Irish girl, you're at the height of the illusion line of the play. This is as far as your hopes are going to carry you. After everything you (and they) have been through, this kiss should have as much kick as a whole scene of physical lovemaking.

This is the key moment of the play. A commitment is being made in the inner story that will inevitably challenge commitments in the outer story. Maire is ready to leave her world for his. Yolland is ready to leave his world for hers. They have an understanding that goes beyond words and a basic misunderstanding that's sure to sink their relationship.

Aren't all lovers like that? Romeo and Juliet have unrealistic hopes about their families. Antony and Cleopatra don't think too clearly about how the rest of the world is going to react to their love. But at least they understand each other. Maire and Yolland are making a lovers' commitment that ignores the real world and their own stated desires.

Can love conquer all? Not when you're in the hands of a clear-eyed playwright. He does not allow you to become fully committed to these lovers. You see too much. And yet, for the moment, at least a piece of you hopes that love can find a way.

The crucial turn in the design of the act now appears in the shape of Sarah, the mute who Manus taught to speak. Here's how the playwright manages it, in stage directions and dialogue.

> *(Pause. Suddenly they kiss. Sarah enters. She sees them. She stands shocked, staring at them. Her mouth works. Then almost to herself.)*
> **SARAH:** Manus...Manus! *(She runs off.)*

You in your privileged seat understand that with one word— "Manus"—the play has changed direction, not just the scene, but the whole movement of the play is pivoting around at the moment of Sarah's look, from the track of illusion to the track of reality. The lovers' commitment has become a threat to commitments held by others. In our terms, the small story is testing the large story. The play is moving from what life might be to what life is fated to be. The key scene has quickly become the turn-around scene.

The playwright could have done this scene (and the entire play) differently. He could have had you understanding one language and not the other. This would put you in Yolland's position, desperate to communicate with a mysterious world. It would give you very little room to play a role separate from Yolland's, and it would make Yolland the center of the play, which, as you will see, he is not. The basic rule of thumb in playwriting is to give the audience more rather than less information. The major tactical playwright decision in *Translations*, to have both Irish and English heard as English, allows you to understand both languages and gives you your godlike powers. It instantly makes you an active player rather than a passive observer.

The stakes are going up. Sarah is running to tell Manus that the English are not only stealing the language, they're stealing the women. Who knows this? Only you. You alone see the immediate threat to the lovers. You brace yourself for the Irish counter-stroke. You who had hopes suddenly have an overwhelming fear for the young innocents you care about.

You have seen what they want. Now you will see what they get.

Second Intermission

Let's step outside for some fresh air. If you're in New York on West 44th or 45th or 46th during intermission, you can look up and down the street at thousands of people crowded under theatre marquees, and you'll hear the buzz produced by powerhouse shows, the kind that make audiences laugh, cry, cheer, and tell their friends that this is one they must see. With the right kind of momentum, a play can run on Broadway for years and make a playwright millions. Well, thousands.

But this doesn't have a lot to do with theatre. Most theatre experiences are about failure. I'm not talking modest lack of success. I mean disaster in large letters. There are few things more deeply depressing than a comedy playing in a house full of empty seats. Maybe leaky lifeboats surrounded by sharks.

I used to think that everything bad that could happen to a playwright had already happened to me. That's an illusion. There's always one more thing that can go wrong. Some people say, "Break a leg," before a show opens. Ever had an actress actually break a leg? I did. Ever have a prominent New York critic walk out in the middle of one of your plays saying loudly to his fellow critics, "Are you staying for the rest of this shit?" I did. Ever have a producer drop dead before he had raised all the money? Yes sir, I did.

Don't get me wrong. We playwrights are proud of our disasters. If we didn't have disaster stories, what would we dine out on? Nevertheless, a playwright has to be careful who he tells his stories to. You can never impress another playwright with your disaster because he/she is sure to have a worse one. Tell about the actor who forgot his lines on opening night and the other playwright shows you the scars from the fallen timbers when the theatre burned down.

I'm not going to tell you about a full-strength disaster. I'll just tell you one more ordinary theatre story. During the first intermission, I told you a sad one. This is a funny one.

In 1977 I wrote a play about two women called *These Men*. My West Coast movie agent loved it. He sent it to an East Coast play agent who also loved it. This agent sold it to Fred Coe, a prominent Broadway producer. Sound good?

Fred Coe brought in his financial partner, Arthur Cantor, to raise the money. We found a good new director and a cast of good new actors. No stars. Fred said, "Ninety-five percent of a producer's work is making three or four crucial decisions—choosing the play, the cast, and a director who won't get in the way. If you make a mistake with one of these, there's nothing you can do to fix it and you'll have a disaster. You are always going to make at least one mistake, you just hope it's a small one."

We started looking for a theatre. It was one of those years when all the Broadway theatres were booked and plays were lined up waiting to get in. The Shuberts offered us the Belasco, a big old house that was much too big for a two-character comedy. We finally found another theatre, but it had a show coming in. But it was a rotten show that wouldn't last very long. But the producer was a rich Hollywood guy who refused to open it and take his lumps and get out. He kept it in previews and kept the playwright rewriting until finally we lost our director to another commitment and decided to wait until the following season.

The following season we found a theatre, small, but still Broadway. I was literally on my way to the Los Angeles airport to fly to New York for the start of rehearsals when my New York agent called to say the theatre had gone bankrupt and the sheriff had padlocked the doors. Some vague story of Mafia involvement I never understood.

We decided to wait one more season, during which time Fred Coe dropped dead, Arthur Cantor backed out, and the new producers couldn't raise the money. Then the show got picked up by a small Off-Off Broadway house (99 seats), where it finally opened in 1980 to bad reviews and died. The theatre stiffed me on my advance, my housing, and my expenses, and I returned to Los Angeles dead broke. My film agent warned me not to talk to anyone about the theatre lest Hollywood people think I was being arrogant. There's always one more thing.

Did I say this was a funny story? I lied. But it's not a story without hope. It turned out *These Men* was not dead. I rewrote it, my daughter took it to England and gave it to an actor who gave it to a director, and a few months later it opened at The Bush (105 seats), a London fringe theatre. I still remember grabbing the papers at seven o'clock the next morning to look at the reviews. *These Men* was a hit. Eight unanimously great reviews. The Sunday *Times* said it should transfer to the West End. A couple of West End producers actually appeared and said they wanted it. Unfortunately they went broke before they could get it on.

The play went to Los Angeles where it was a huge hit at the Los Angeles Actors Theatre (39 seats) and played for eight months. Then it went to the Magic Theatre in San Francisco (110 seats) where again it was a huge hit. Then four different producers in London optioned it for the West End, but none could get it going. Then it started playing in tiny theatres in Germany, Austria, Italy, then London again...

And in this way twenty years passed.

What did I get out of it? A few dollars. Some brilliant reviews. A poster on my wall. Never a run in a commercial house in any country. Of course, during that time I wrote other plays. One was immediately optioned for Broadway—

Wait, the lights are blinking. You have to get back for the last act. Next time I really will tell you a funny story about the theatre. I promise.

Ends

There is a scene in the play *Strider*, in which a decrepit old Russian Prince comes to visit a horse farm. As he walks about with the young Count who owns the farm, he passes a mangy old horse tied to a stake. The horse stares at the Prince, and after a while the Prince looks back at the horse. Only you notice this exchange of looks. If this were the beginning of the play you would be gathering your privileged information and assuming your role of analyzing, evaluating, and anticipating. You would not be passive in your privileged seat, but you would be cool.

In fact, this scene takes place at the end of the play, and your role has changed dramatically. If it's been a good production, at this moment you are leaning forward in your seat, not just hoping for, but demanding a specific action. There is something up there on the stage you—must—see.

The playwright has you in his grip. He's worked for two hours to get you to this point, and now a dance of exquisite tension begins between you and the stage. There is something you want. You demand it. You beg for it. You got to have it. Am I talking about theatre or sex? Actually, this is about as close to sex as you're going to get without sex. The play-wright is putting you through agony and you love it, because in the end you know you're going to get it.

Strider is one of the purest examples I know of the audience-playwright dance at the end of a play. It began as a story by Tolstoy that was turned into a Russian play and then into an American musical by Mark Rozovsky and brought to Broadway in 1974. *Strider* is about the last day in the life of an old horse who has been returned to the farm where he was born. He's going to be slaughtered in the morning. He doesn't know it. You do.

As in all plays, there are two worlds. Here they appear to be the world of animals and the world of humans. Each speaks a separate language. You, of course, in your privileged seat, understand both. But the human-animal distinction is not really the key. In an early scene, one of the horses says: "We know how to love. We're animals." Later in the play there are humans who also know how to love the animal way, which puts them in the same world.

Then there is Strider, a horse who is gelded and can no longer love that way, and so moves from the world of animal love to the world of another kind of love. The universe of the play is split between love that takes and love that gives. The play is the encounter between them.

On his last day, the old horse, not knowing his fate (innocent, vulner-able, every moment precious), recalls his life. The play is framed by a scene in a gypsy encampment, and Strider's story is sung and narrated by gypsies, which gives our imagination a shove in the right direction and provides a screen for what could be some embarrassment over actors playing talking horses.

The unique thing about Strider is that he was born a piebald, thought ugly and useless and rejected by everyone. He's desperate to find someone to love. You, in your privileged seat, understand the realities of life that the innocent horse does not. He lives his horse illusions about the world, learning about animal love just in time to be gelded. When he loses the power to engage in animal love, he loses one of the great pleasures in the physical world, but (he tells us) he gains something in the world of the spirit—"a clear vision of the true relationships between all living things." Since he is just a horse (and a doomed horse at that) he is still innocent about a lot of things, which allows you to maintain your role of understanding what he does not.

Strider is bought by the dashing Prince and his life begins as a carriage horse. The Prince understands him, talks to him, calls him friend. Strider can see the Prince fears no one and loves only himself, and therefore (the horse understands his own psychology) Strider falls in love with him (key scene) and will do anything to please him (inner story). The Prince puts him in a race and he wins (outer story). This is the high point of Strider's life and the top of the illusion line of the play.

A moment later, the Prince's mistress disappears from the racetrack with another man. The Prince makes Strider chase after them. Strider breaks down (turn-around scene, fate line begins). The Prince gets rid of him. He goes from one cruel owner to another. Finally—old, sick, useless— he's brought back to the horse farm. He doesn't know he's about to die. He thinks someone is coming "to doctor [him]." You in your privileged seat see the threat that he does not (urgency), even as you hope that somehow he will be saved.

The Prince enters with the young Count. Years have passed. The Prince is old and drunk, reduced to the job of buying horses for the government. The young Count is showing horses to him. The Prince notices Strider, tied to the stake. The horse recognizes the only human he's ever loved. Does the Prince recognize the horse? "How piebald that one is. I had a piebald once, exactly like him," says the Prince. You lean forward with hope.

Instead of remembering the horse, the Prince thinks about his own past dissolute life and his squandered fortune. The Count wants to show him more horses. Suddenly the Prince's memories change. He remembers his pleasures, the pure joy of horse racing: "...I once had a trotter, a well-bred piebald gelding. Something like this poor wreck." The horse looks at the Prince. Does he recognize him now? The Prince continues, "Oh, what a horse he was!" You in the audience are thinking: "At last, he'll recognize Strider, buy him, and save him."

The Prince continues talking about the horse's speed and strength and beauty. He tries to remember his name. You urge him on from your seat: "Yes, Prince, remember his name!" And then he does remember: "Strider! That was his name." Thank God, he remembers! You're ready to cheer until the Prince continues: "He resembled this poor thing. There aren't horses like him anymore..." He retreats into drunken memories of his golden youth, getting people and times mixed up, forgetting the horse who stares at him forlornly.

The audience is getting desperate. You recognize the horse. Why can't the Prince recognize the horse? (You may not think about it until after the play, but eventually it will strike you that the old Prince resists recognizing the broken-down Strider because then he will also have to face his own broken-down life.) It's no longer a question of saving Strider. You know the horse is old and sick; he's going to die soon. All you want—and want desperately—is for the Prince to recognize the horse who loves him.

The Prince collapses into boozy confusion between past and present. "I used to keep others," he tells the servant who tries to help him, "now others keep me." Then he looks one more time at the horse. "It's really amazing how much this poor wreck resembles Strider."

By now you're ready to jump out of your seat and shout at the stage: "*It's him! It's him!*" The sick old Prince and the sick old horse look at each other. The horse nestles his head on the Prince's shoulder and brushes his cheek. The two are fixed in a moment of recognition so sad and so touching that you may find yourself weeping. The Prince reaches out, as though to embrace Strider. Is he moving from the world of selfish love to the world of another kind of love? He stops, repelled by the mangy horse. "No," he says, backing away. "No." But you know that he knows it's Strider.

The horse has been recognized and perhaps, for a fraction of a second, his love has been returned. The Prince has faced his own life, and you have looked directly into the heart of another person. This doesn't happen very often in the real world. It can happen every night in the theatre.

What if the Prince had said, "Yes, that's him," and then wept? What would happen to your role? It would evaporate. Sure, you would get what you demanded, but not in a form that would let you play your part. You would no longer be seeing below the surface of things, understanding what others do not—or will not—admit. All you could do now—at the end of the play—would be to observe, and if the Prince was weeping for himself you would not weep for him, that role being occupied. In fact, you might adopt the role of being slightly embarrassed at the sentimental absurdity of a man and a horse embracing.

One more point: Isn't it curious that when the Prince says "No" you so clearly hear "Yes"? In life, you're generally not that clever. In the theatre, the playwright leaves a space for your insight, and he has an actor to point you in the right direction. When King Lear, speaking defiantly to his cruel daughters, says—

> I will have such revenges on you both
> That all the world shall—I will do such things—
> What they are, yet I know not; but they shall be
> The terrors of the earth.

—the actor uses voice and body language to convert Lear's bravado into pathos, so that you can nod sagely and think: "Oh, that poor old man."

Let's look at some of the other plays we've talked about and see how your role changes at the end. Remember, the middle of the play tends to be about what the characters want; the end tends to be about what they get. The middle has the turn-around scene, where illusion meets reality and commitments test each other, raising your hopes and fears for the innocent and vulnerable people you care about; the end has the consequences, followed often by a moment of self-knowledge, and then the final action where the main character, having moved from one world to another, makes his choice and pays the price.

Romeo and Juliet begins as a hopeful play about the triumph of young love, until Romeo, trying to stop a fight between the warring factions, kills Juliet's cousin Tybalt (turn-around scene), and the play pivots from the track of hope and illusion to the track of reality and fate. Romeo is banished from Verona to Mantua; Juliet will be forced to marry Paris the following Thursday (urgency).

Their illusions do not die easily. Friar Laurence, who married them, organizes a plot to bring the separated lovers together. You know the ending, the chorus told you at the beginning of the play. And yet you still hope that the lovers can be reunited. The friar's plan involves a potion that will make Juliet appear to be dead long enough for her to be discovered, mourned, and then buried in the Capulet family vault. Meanwhile, the friar will send a message to Romeo telling him to come to the tomb. Together they will wait for Juliet to awaken and then the reunited young lovers can run off to Mantua.

Juliet drinks the potion. Romeo gets a message, but it's the wrong message. His servant comes from Verona to tell him that Juliet is dead, while the Friar's messenger is delayed. Romeo comes to the Capulet burial vault. He has bought poison so he can die at Juliet's side. He kills Paris who gets in his way. Romeo opens the tomb to look at Juliet's body.

What do you desperately want?

You want her to wake up! Or you want Friar Laurence to get there in time to stop Romeo from taking the poison. You know it won't happen, and still you demand that the young lovers be re-united.

What do you get?

Romeo takes the poison and dies. The Friar enters with Romeo's servant too late. Juliet wakes up, sees the dead Romeo, and stabs herself to death. Bad timing all around.

Didn't quite get what you demanded, did you? But—and this is always the crucial question—are you content with what you got?

Romeo and Juliet are dead. They made their commitments, had moments of self-knowledge, lived their choices, and paid the price. How can the playwright make this acceptable to the audience that wants them to live? First of all, you knew it was coming. While it looked like a play about the triumph of love, you knew it would turn into a tragedy of circumstance. Then it takes one more turn. In death, the lovers are reunited, and in death they triumph. The family hatreds that destroyed Romeo and Juliet will now die. Enemies will reconcile. Love will replace hate.

Are you content? The kids are dead, but there is hope for other kids who will come after them. There is also the common youthful fantasy that adults will destroy them because they don't understand them, and then they'll be sorry. This is what happens in *Romeo and Juliet*, so if you're young there is a special kind of see-I-told-you pleasure in the ending. If you're older, you will note that Romeo and Juliet will never age. Juliet will not get wrinkles. Romeo will not get prostate cancer. The disappointments of life will not touch them (as they touch you). Romeo and Juliet and their love will be forever young. Does that leave you happy? No. Content? Yes.

Oedipus the King is a tough play about which to ask, "Is there something the audience demands to see at the end?"

I guess you could say, "I want Oedipus to wake up and find out it's all been a horrible dream." But as you've known from the beginning (even before the beginning if you're an ancient Athenian), Oedipus himself is the murderer he seeks and the cause of the plague in his city (outer story), and he is the son of the murdered king and has married his own mother (inner story). Jocasta, his wife/mother, is the first (after you) to understand all this. Distraught, she runs into the palace. Then Oedipus, having forced the truth from the shepherd, also runs into the palace. Now he knows what you've known all along.

Play over? Well, no. What more do you want? You've sat there with god-like calm, knowing that when Oedipus curses the murderer he is cursing himself, and knowing the added horrors that are in store for him. What's left that you truly demand to see?

The end begins with a messenger bringing news from the palace. Jocasta has hung herself and Oedipus has poked his eyes out. What if the messenger came out and said that Jocasta has hung herself, and when Oedipus found out, he hung himself too and that's what happens when you don't accept what the gods decree. Play over; go home. Happy now?

No, you're not. Your role has changed. You've invested a lot in Oedipus, and you want to see what's become of him. You may even secretly relish the thought of looking at the final humiliation of the proud and arrogant man who placed himself above the gods (and ordinary people like you).

The messenger ends his speech telling the chorus (and you) that Oedipus wants himself shown to all of Thebes as a father murderer and a mother—well, you know. You focus on the big doors of the palace. "The great doors are opening," says the messenger—"you are about to see a sight, a horror even his mortal enemy would pity."

Oedipus enters, led by a boy. He stands at the palace steps, as he did at the beginning of the play. But, oh, the change. He's gone from the greatest man in the city to the lowest—a blind, bloody, helpless criminal. What did the Athenian audience feel when they saw him? First terror, just as Aristotle says, terror that if the gods could decree this for Oedipus they could decree it for anyone, including the Athenian audience.

You, the modern audience, are not so worried about the prophecies of the gods, but fear of fate is still part of our modern lives. So, safe in your privileged place, you can also feel a bit of terror. And maybe just a touch of self-satisfaction. He didn't deserve everything he got, but he sure did make it worse.

Have you had enough? No, you demand more. Even in his agony, even as he flays himself in public, Oedipus still seems the same headstrong man he was before, only now the object of his anger is himself. You want to see change. Not just the outward change from king to beggar, but inner change as well. You are looking for the moment of self-knowledge.

The chorus asks Oedipus what drove him to tear out his eyes, and he says:

> Apollo, friend, Apollo—he ordained
> my agonies—

He admits something he has never admitted before: The god is in charge, not him. With eyes, Oedipus was blind. Blind, he sees. Oedipus continues, "But the hand that struck my eyes was mine." This is a crucial point. The gods control our destiny; we control our response to it. That's why *Oedipus the King* is a play. If we controlled nothing, there would be no point in watching *Oedipus the King* or any play. At the end, a play must contain inner change as well as outer change. Inner change involves choices. Sometimes the choices are narrow, but they are choices nevertheless.

Consider Iphigenia in Euripides' play, *Iphigenia at Aulis*. She's about to be sacrificed (urgency) to the god Artemis by her father Agamemnon (inner story), so the winds will blow and the Greek fleet can sail to Troy and fight the Trojans (outer story).

When she arrives at Aulis, Iphigenia thinks she's come as a bride for Achilles (innocent, vulnerable) You, godlike, know the truth. You watch with fear and hope as her mother Clytemnestra tries to save her. Finally the young and delicate Iphigenia pitifully begs her father not to sacrifice her. "A poor life is better than a grand death." Agamemnon will not be moved. "It is Hellas for whom I must, whether I wish or not, offer you as sacrifice. I can not resist the claim of country."

Iphigenia's last hope is the great warrior Achilles who promised to save her but proves too weak to face all the Greeks who want her killed. Iphigenia is trapped. There is no escape. Does she have choices? If the answer is no, then there's no play.

Iphigenia has the choice of running and hiding until she is caught and dragged by her hair to be killed, or the choice of sitting and weeping until she is dragged by her hair to be killed, or—and what a stunning choice—she can turn to face her pursuers and say calmly: "I must die? All right, then I am resolved to die." You hoped that a scared young girl would be saved. You get a woman who has come to self-knowledge and chooses to accept her fate with dignity. Stirred by her courage, you may find yourself in tears.

Back to Oedipus: it seems that he can run away, cower, or kill himself. Instead, he chooses to embrace his fate. He's moving from the world of the skeptic who believes that a strong man can control events, to acceptance of a world ruled by the gods.

This is a harsh school for Oedipus. In his arrogance and pride he tried to run from the gods' judgment, which only made things worse for him. Now, in front of the whole world, he admits to being "the great blasphemer."

Creon appears, and you can tell from Oedipus' attitude toward his brother-in-law/uncle how far he's come in understanding. Creon and Oedipus are paired. Creon has honored the gods as much as Oedipus has disdained them. The last time they were together, Oedipus screamed at Creon, accusing him of plotting to overthrow him. Now he submits to his authority. Oedipus is not craven. He does not pity himself. He is, in fact, pitiless on himself, and that allows the Athenian audience, and you, to feel pity for him.

Oedipus has moved from one world to another. He has dropped his illusions. He has faced reality. He has come to self-knowledge. He will act as the gods decree: "I have been saved for something great and terrible, something strange. Well let my destiny come and take me on its way." This is what you demanded, and you have it. The Athenian audience (according to Aristotle) went home purged of pity and terror. Does the modern audience do the same? What do you think?

In the turn-around scene of *Born Yesterday*, Billie Dawn, the ex-chorus cutie, refuses to sign a paper for Harry Brock, the millionaire junk man. At this point, inner and outer stories challenge each other. Even though she lives off Harry and is afraid of him, Billie's learned some things about ethics from Paul, the idealistic reporter, and she won't sign anything she hasn't read, thus blocking Harry's crooked business deal. He slaps her twice; she sobs and signs.

One moment—two slaps—turns both outer and inner stories around. It has seemed to be a play about a businessman who pushes everyone around to promote a crooked deal (outer story). It's turning into a play about an ex-chorus girl and a reporter trying to stop him, during which the ex-chorus girl goes through a metamorphosis (inner story).

The slap not only changes Billie, it changes you. Up to this point you've been amused by Harry. You hate to admit it, but you may even find yourself secretly admiring his anything-goes, take-no-prisoners business philosophy. You recognize that in his crude way he loves Billie. At least she's a possession he wants to keep. And in her way she has feelings for him. You may actually wonder if they might have a future together. Maybe if she changed a little and he changed a lot...

When Harry hits Billie, everything changes. You hate what Harry's done and you know exactly what you want to see now. In the outer story, you want Harry's deal to fall apart and you want him caught and punished. In the inner story, you want to see Billie leave Harry for Paul, the idealistic reporter. And you want her to realize who she really is, and to act on that knowledge.

The slap is the moment where illusions run into reality. Now come the consequences. Harry orders the sobbing Billie out of the room and she leaves, defeated yet defiant. Harry thinks he's won again, but something has happened to Billie. She is moving from his world to another world. Harry doesn't see it. You do.

Act three: Billie has not returned. Harry is worried about her, though he won't admit it. He probably even feels a little remorseful, though he would certainly never admit that. Harry's lawyer is worried because, on paper, Billie owns everything Harry has. Only one way out: Harry has to marry her. He feels trapped. He also doesn't want to lose her.

Billie and Paul appear and steal papers that will incriminate Harry. Paul wants to marry Billie. She puts him off (for the moment).

Billie has moved from the world of the predators to the world of the good citizens. The question is, how far has she come in her inner journey? The playwright gives you a way to figure that out for yourself.

After Paul leaves with the papers, Harry appears. He's remorseful in his own way. He tells Billie they are finished with Paul and education. "It gets in my way—and I don' like you upset so much. It's bad for you."

Then Harry asks her to marry him. Actually, he tells her they're going to get married. Now this is not one of those plays where the main character has to choose between love and everything else—as happens in *Romeo and Juliet* and *Antony and Cleopatra*—allowing you to measure just how much love is worth. In *Born Yesterday*, Billie's choices are easy. She wants Harry defeated and she wants Paul, and you can guess which way the play is going. Inner and outer stories will ultimately work together. This is a simpler structural arrangement than in *Romeo and Juliet* or *Antony and Cleopatra*, where the characters pay a heavy price for their choices. Here, it's win-win for Billie.

So why are you still sitting there watching the play? Because there's something you want, and you're not going to leave the theatre until you get it.

Harry has spent his life slapping people around. You want to know if Billie has come far enough—not just in becoming a good citizen, but in understanding herself—to do something about it. In other words, you want to see the worm turn.

Billie starts the sequence with a curt "No" to Harry's marriage proposal.

That's good news. She knows her own mind now. But is that what you're demanding? Not quite.

Harry is astonished. Nobody who depends on him turns him down. "How can you not wanna marry me?"

Billie tells him he's too dumb. Getting better. She's no longer scared of the big bully. But you're still not satisfied. You want more.

Harry's baffled. He doesn't understand what he's done to deserve all this. Okay, he talked rough to her now and then, and sure he slapped her around a couple of times, but is that a reason for this attitude? If there's a problem, can't they straighten it out?

"No," says Billie. "Why not?" he asks.

Okay, here it comes. The speech of the play, where Billie defines Harry and, more importantly, herself. She talks about her education. It didn't come from the books Paul gave her, they just confused her. But when Harry hit her, that's when she realized what it all means. Some people are givers and some are takers. And that's not fair. "So I'm not gonna let you anymore. *Or anybody else!*"

Billie has discovered exactly who she is, and nobody is ever going to push her around again. The worm has turned. She has come to self-knowledge and she has acted. If you're like most audiences, this is where you cheer.

After the key moment in the second act of *Oleanna*—the revelation of the student's complaint to the Tenure Committee—the professor wriggles like a fish on a hook. He says he wants to help the student before the situation escalates and she's humiliated. She answers curtly: "I don't think I need your help."

Speaking for herself and her "Group," she lists his crimes: sexist and demeaning remarks. That vile story—"*classist,* and *manipulative* and *pornographic.*" When he tries to answer, she interrupts him, just as he interrupted her in the previous act. What gives him the right to play the classroom patriarch, to grant this, to deny that? To call higher education a joke. To mock the hardworking students who slave to come to this school?

He argues back with quiet desperation, still the teacher appealing to reason. He's not an exploiter and she's not deranged. They don't have to fight. Sure, people are self-serving. People are imperfect. But they can still discuss their differences in their own words, like two fallible human beings.

For a moment she almost seems persuaded. She begins to talk without the militant phrases of her Group. Usually you feel for the trapped and vulnerable. But perhaps he has been a bit paternal, not sensitive enough to her struggles, even a bit flirtatious. Maybe she is a victim, though not the kind of victim she claims. You feel a flicker of hope for both of them. Perhaps they can both learn something.

Another phone call from his wife interrupts them. Again the house, the deposit, the lawyer, the deal. He tells her the house sale will go through and he's dealing with the complaint.

By the time he gets off the phone the moment is lost. The student says politely they will talk about their differences at the Tenure Committee hearing (which will cause him to lose his house and the deposit).

Flustered, he tries to keep the conversation going. She insists on leaving. He puts his hands on her. "I have no desire to *hold* you, I just want to *talk* to you." She screams. It's a moment of stunning surprise. But why?

The play has been carefully organized so that it seems to exist only in the world of educated talk. The last thing you anticipated in a professor's office was a physical action, even a small one denied by his words.

You want to yell down at him: "*Let her go!*" But it's too late. The play is turning around on its axis. His once secure life is shattering. The outer story of a professor and a student is being challenged by the inner story of a man and woman. The track of illusion is turning into the track of reality. You dread the consequences that will follow.

Act three: Same setting, same people. The fight is over. The professor is broken, sad, beyond sad. He has asked to see the student once more. She sits opposite him, the prim commissar: "What do you want to tell me?"

He wants to talk about the accusations. She corrects him. Not accusations. Facts. He has been found guilty on the facts. He will not get tenure. He will no longer have a job. She is the teacher, and he's the slow student. She lectures him:

> You don't understand? You're angry? What has *led* you to this place? Not your sex. Not your race. Not your class. YOUR OWN ACTIONS. And you're *angry*. You *ask* me here. What *do* you want? You want to "charm" me. You want to "convince"

me. You want me to recant. I will *not* recant. Why should I...? What I say is right. You tell me, you are going to tell me that you have a wife and child. You are going to say that you have a career and that you've worked for twenty years for this. Do you know what you've *worked* for? *Power*. For *power*. Do you understand? And you sit there, and you tell me stories. About your *house*, about all the private *schools*, and about *privilege*, and how you are entitled. To *buy*, to *spend*, to *mock*, to *summon*. All your stories. All your silly weak *guilt*, it's all about *privilege*, and you won't know it. Don't you see? You worked twenty years for the right to *insult* me. And you feel entitled to be *paid* for it. Your home. Your wife...Your sweet "deposit" on your house...

She's humiliating him. You wait for his response. If you are part of the middle-of-the-road audience, your blood pressure is rising. You may be feeling little men with hammers banging on your skull. You don't want the professor to engage the student in more discussion. Or even to answer her. *You want him to do something*. And if he doesn't *do something* you may come down out of your seat and *do something* yourself.

What does he do? He begs. "Don't you have feelings?" he says.

Feelings don't interest her. She has a responsibility to speak for all those who have suffered as she has suffered from his exploitation. She strips him of everything he has lived by. He claims to believe in free intellectual discourse. He believes in nothing. She spits out words from her new vocabulary. He believes in an elitist protected hierarchy that rewards him and for which he is the clown.

As your fury grows, she continues with his humiliation. She knows what he thinks of her. He thinks she's a frightened, repressed, confused, abandoned young thing of some doubtful sexuality who wants power and revenge. Isn't it true? The veneer of professor talk falls away. "Yes," he says simply. "I do."

She tells him this is the first moment that he has treated her with respect. The truth is he hates her because she has power. And if he thinks she's cruel, he should understand how students feel about the power the school has over them. One word from a professor can destroy everything a student has worked for. Now he knows what it's like to be subject to that power.

She's still not finished. She wants him to confess his crimes. They go over the evidence. The touch on her shoulder when they first met? Wearily he says: "It was devoid of sexual content." "I say it was not," she shouts in his face. "I SAY IT WAS NOT. Don't you begin to *see*...? Don't you begin to understand? *It's not for you to say.*"

You want to shake him. You demand that he fight back. But he's groveling, compromising, willing to say anything to appease her. Yes, he's beginning to understand—the way the re-educated prisoner begins to understand that it was all his fault—Stalin was right, the trial was right, the rigged evidence was right, the fake confession was right. He apologizes to the student, like the prisoner apologizing to the Commissar for the torture.

You feel like your eyes are bulging out—and she's still not finished. She wants the professor to understand her. She is waiting to be thanked for destroying him. The professor is exhausted. All the life has drained out of him.

"What's the use," he says. "It's over."

Not quite. Incredibly, she offers him (and you) one last sliver of hope. As she turns to leave, she says, "What if it were possible that my Group withdraws its complaint?"

You think, "My God, could this nightmare really be over?" Warily the professor asks the price. She hands him a list of books her Group finds "questionable." He finds his own book on the list. Do they want him to ban his own book?

No, not "banned," she says, merely "removed."

Pause for thought: Each scene in a play contains a test of character, and usually, as the play develops through stroke and counter-stroke, the tests escalate. At this point, after all his humiliations, when he seems completely defenseless, now come the professor's last tests, his final exam.

The professor has been offered a way out. Is he willing to pay the price? You know what you desperately want him to do, but you fear he lacks the courage to do it.

To the student he says simply: "Get out of here." He has a responsibility to himself, his children, and his profession. If it has cost him his job, maybe the job wasn't worth having. Hooray! A bit of self-knowledge at last. But it's not enough. You demand more. A lot more.

The professor discovers from a phone call to his lawyer that he's going to be charged with attempted rape. Will this send him over the top? Is this the final, final test? Not yet.

He telephones his wife and tells her everything is going to be all right. Before he hangs up, he calls her "baby." The student tells him not to call his wife "baby."

And with this, the professor exits the world of talk. He hits the student. He beats her. He knocks her to the floor. He calls her "cunt." Then he picks up a chair and advances toward her.

Is he going to smash her head open? Will that satisfy you? You wanted violence. You got violence. How much more do you want?

In the moment that he stands over her, chair in the air, you may have second thoughts. In fact, you may be shocked. Shocked at the professor. Shocked at yourself.

He sets the chair down. You are relieved. Yes, you wanted it, but you never thought...It may take a few moments to realize that *Oleanna* has moved you from being a middle-of-the-road audience with a godlike role of understanding to a mob that wants blood.

I have to note here that at the world premiere of *Oleanna* in Cambridge, a friend who attended reported that the audience was violently split. Men argued with women. Husbands with wives. Old with young. Some wanted the student shot as a rabid animal, and some wanted the professor put in jail and maybe burned at the stake.

After everybody's passions have cooled, it will be time to reflect on what has really happened here. Who is the oppressor? Who is the victim? And a more basic question: Is rational discussion of the issues still possible?

What does the playwright want from you now—all of you—no matter what you believe about the play? He wants you to sit back and think.

In the key moment of *The Seagull*, Nina, the innocent country girl, kisses Trigorin, the famous novelist. The consequences of this moment will alter both inner and outer stories, as life and art become entangled. Nina will leave Konstantin, the aspiring young writer who loves her, to be with Trigorin in Moscow and seek fame as an actress. Trigorin will leave his mistress, Arkadina, the famous actress who is Konstantin's mother.

You hope for Nina's happiness; you also fear for a passionate innocent running off with a middle-aged writer who sees her as an interesting subject for a story. Not a great formula for happiness, you say to yourself during the intermission.

The final act begins after the passage of two years. Nina is no longer with Trigorin. She had a baby, the baby died, Trigorin abandoned her. Somewhere during that time there was a turn-around scene where illusion met reality and the play changed course. That's a scene you don't get to see. Why not?

Why not show the tacky hotel where Nina learns that Trigorin is leaving her pregnant, or with a baby, or having just lost a baby. Would he be cold and off-hand? Would she be hysterical?

Chekhov doesn't like these kinds of scenes. He shies away from confrontation on the stage (unless he can screen it with comedy). He prefers showing the results of confrontation and letting you imagine the rest. If you actually watched Trigorin leaving Nina, there would not be much for you to do except avert your eyes from the pain.

Other factors: Chekhov wants to preserve the unity of the play. He wants to keep it all in the country and leave the city as a place of dreams. And he wants to preserve Trigorin as a somewhat sympathetic figure, the detached intelligent writer. Dramatizing the turn-around scene with all its cruelty would leave you actively hating Trigorin.

Dealing only with the consequences of the scene also preserves your role. It makes you work a little to catch up with what has happened to all the characters on the estate after the passage of two years.

Trigorin and Arkadina have returned. They are together again. The famous writer and the famous actress continue to prosper, suffering nothing and thinking only of themselves. Trigorin is writing a new story, possibly about Nina. Konstantin still lives on the estate. He's become a writer. Arkadina never has time to read his stories. She would rather talk (a little too insistently) about her latest stage triumph.

They have had some news about Nina. She is an actress, though (according to reports) not a very good one. You are anxious to find out what's happened to her and if the changes in her will affect others.

So, middle of act four; night. Konstantin is at his desk, trying to write, anguished that his art, like his life, is cold and arid. He hears a sound in the garden, goes out, and returns with Nina, who puts her head on his chest and sobs. They are both dazed and distraught, like two ship-wrecked sailors. For a moment they talk freely about what's become of their lives. She wanted fame and glory; he wanted to create new forms of literature.

Reality has replaced illusion for both of them. Nina is a provincial actress, traveling third class on trains with peasants, going from town to town where "the educated merchants will pester me with their attentions. It's a coarse life."

Konstantin listens to her intimate revealing talk and reveals his own unhappiness. "Ever since I lost you, and my work began to be published, my life has been unbearable—I am miserable..." He declares his love for her: "I call to you, I kiss the ground you walked on..."

Listening to him, you suddenly think: My God, could it be that their adversities are drawing them together? Is it possible, after all this time, they will fall into each other's arms? Hopes rising, you lean forward in your seat until Nina, confused, says to herself: "Why does he talk like that, why does he talk like that?"

Konstantin doesn't hear her. You do. The scene pivots around with your realization that they are still two mismatched people talking past each other. This allows space for you to play your godlike role of understanding them both and seeing, sadly and finally, that there is no hope for them as lovers (inner story); which raises the crucial question of the final act: Are there any hopes for them, if not in their disastrous personal lives, then as artists (outer story)?

Konstantin begs Nina to stay with him or to let him go with her. Nina's feverish mind wanders back to her bitter life with Trigorin, how he made fun of her dreams and how badly she performed on the stage. Then she says, "I'm not like that now...Now I'm a real actress."

With that statement, the foundation is laid for the change in your role at the end of *The Seagull.* You've been the good detective—evaluating and anticipating, feeling hopes and fears for people you care about, understanding what others don't. Now you want to know if what Nina says about herself is true. Has suffering turned her into an artist? Looked at analytically, you want to know how the inner story has affected the outer story. In an earlier scene, Konstantin commented on Nina's acting abilities:

> ...She always attempted big parts, but she acted crudely, taste-lessly, with stiff gestures and strident intonations. There were moments when she showed talent—when she uttered a cry or had a dying scene—but those were only moments.

A bad actor with "moments." This may say more about Konstantin's bitterness than about Nina's abilities.

So whose judgment can you take? Trigorin is the real artist in the play. He judges the faults in Konstantin's writing—"and not one living character"—and you believe him. Nina reports that Trigorin ridiculed her acting, but then he didn't believe in the theatre, and you can guess that the idealistic Nina probably began to annoy him.

What about Arkadina? She's the famous actress who encouraged Nina in act one. Now she says nothing. Perhaps she hasn't forgiven Nina for her affair with Trigorin. Or perhaps she has no interest in Nina's acting abilities because she doesn't think much of them.

As for relying on Nina's judgment of herself, theatre audiences are ornery. When someone on the stage tells you how terrific he is at something, you tend to back off and think, "Well, maybe you are, and maybe you aren't."

Is Nina a real actress now? You desperately hope that she has salvaged something from her suffering that can make her life bearable. Not only do you want to know, but—and here your role changes dramatically—you want proof.

The theatre teaches through strong contrasts. You saw Nina performing Konstantin's play in act one—a young sweet non-professional reciting strange, almost nonsensical lines on a makeshift stage by the lake: "Men, lions, eagles, and partridges, horned deer, geese, spiders, silent fish that dwell in the deep..."

Was she a real actress then? Probably not. Is there any way you can find out if she's a real actress now?

Anguished and distraught, she's about to leave Konstantin's room. He begs her to stay. In their last precious moment together, she confesses her love for Trigorin. No matter what he has done she loves him passionately, desperately. She is down to the very depths of her misery. Can anything be salvaged? Is there anything that can give her tortured life meaning?

Has she become a real actress?

Her feverish mind transports her (and you) back to that first performance. You remember the evening, the people, the moonlight, the stage, the lake. You lean forward. You know what you want, and you want it now. The playwright has you in his grip. Nina pauses. She says to Konstantin (and to you): "Do you remember?" Oh, yes, yes, yes, you remember. Then, as you hold your breath, she recites:

> Men, lions, eagles, and partridges, horned deer, geese, spiders,
> silent fish that dwell in the deep, starfish, and creatures invisible

to the eye—these and all living things, all, all living things, having completed their sad cycle, are no more...For thousands of years the earth has borne no living creature. And now in vain this poor moon lights her lamp. Cranes no longer wake and cry in meadows, May beetles are heard no more in the linden groves...

So? Well? Is she a real actress now?

There's no one to give you guidance. No tears, no cheers, no Hollywood montage to show her name in lights while her heart is breaking. Here in the theatre, in your privileged seat, you have to judge for yourself.

A lot depends on the approach of the actor, who can let Nina's suffering play through the speech, so the words are deeper, richer, "better." Or the actor can play Nina's feverish distracted mind and make the speech "worse." I talked to a director who said, "The issue is not whether she's better or worse. The speech has to be true to the character and the situation."

True, yes, but many actresses try to give the speech a depth of understanding Nina did not possess at the beginning of the play, and many directors think that if Nina were no better than she had been, or even worse, that might be too much for the audience to bear. Still the question will persist in your mind: Can you really tell if Nina is an actress?

In Mike Nichols' 2001 production at the Shakespeare Theater in New York's Central Park, the actress did not try to "act" the lines. She commented on them ironically, nostalgically, thus leaving the acting question moot.

A lesser play, like *Born Yesterday*, gives you exactly what you demand.

The worm turns. Harry Brock gets his. Billie will marry the reporter and—well, who can say? But who's asking? It's a well-made play and it leaves you happy.

A contemporary play like *Oleanna* seduces you into demanding violence and then leaves you with an after-taste of guilt, as it swings you around and makes you look at yourself.

With Nina you knew what you wanted—but what did you get? After everything that's happened you still may not be sure. Will Chekhov leave her with something that gives meaning to her life and gives you some certainty? If he didn't, people would not be coming to see this play a hundred years after it was written.

What does Chekhov do? He shifts the question and gives a different answer. Before Nina leaves Konstantin, she says in measured words:

> I know now, I understand, that in our work, Kostya—whether it's acting or writing—what's important is not fame, not glory, not the things I used to dream of, but the ability to endure. To be able to bear one's cross and have faith. I have faith, and it's not so painful now, and when I think of my vocation, I'm not afraid of life.

Chekhov has reframed the question of the outer story from, "Can she act?" to a question in the inner story, "Can she live?"

You have looked into the soul of a vulnerable and innocent human being. You've seen her make choices. You've seen her take the consequences. You've seen her endure pain and suffering and come to self-knowledge. When Nina says calmly and quietly that she's not afraid of life, you believe her.

*   *   *

In the key scene of *Translations*, George Yolland, the English officer, kisses Maire, the Irish farm girl. They are observed by Sarah, the mute who has begun to speak. She sees the kiss and runs off calling for Manus, the country schoolteacher who loves Maire and hates the English troops. This is the moment of the turn-around.

You have hopes for the young lovers, but you fear the consequences, as the commitment sealed by the kiss (inner story) tests the commitment of the Irish determined to protect their world from the English (outer story). At this point it seems like a variation of the *Romeo and Juliet* design—young love destroyed by feuding families. In *Romeo and Juliet* the key scene of the kiss comes some time before the turn-around caused by Romeo killing Juliet's cousin Tybalt. In *Translations* the turn-around follows the key action immediately.

Notice how the characters here are inter-related. Lt. Yolland doesn't have to kill anyone to arouse the Irish; one kiss observed is enough. Sarah reports to Manus, and then Manus—well, you'll have to guess what Manus does, but even now you know it's going to be bad for somebody. What happens to people in one story always affects people in the other story.

Thus far, it has looked like a romance between a young English soldier and a young Irish girl against the background of English-Irish conflict. Now it will turn into something quite different, as the play changes course from the track of hope and illusion to the track of reality and fate. Your role is also changing. You know what you want and you know what you fear. Soon you are going to start making demands.

Act three, scene one: Manus is packing; he's on his way somewhere. Not to the teaching post he talked about, someplace else—and in a hurry. But where? And why? You feel that something has happened here. But what?

Sarah and Manus' brother, Owen the translator, watch. Usually you're ahead of the people on the stage. You know what they don't. Sometimes they know what you don't, and you scramble to catch up. The design of the play keeps you in constant motion.

So who's going to tell you what's happened? You have seen the escalating strokes and counter-strokes between Irish and English. You've seen the kiss. You've seen the call for Manus. The playwright has you in his grip. He can let the story spin out a bit to increase the tension.

Owen is still doing the work of changing Irish place names to English and putting the results in the Name-Book. He's doing it alone—no Yolland. Aware that something has occurred, Owen warns Manus about running away. "Clear out now and Lancey'll think you're involved somehow." You think: "Involved in what?" Your heart sinks as Owen reassures Manus that Yolland may have just gone off to one of the islands for a bit of adventure, or maybe he's lying drunk in a ditch somewhere. When one character on the stage reassures a second character about a missing third character, you know something bad has happened.

Manus leaves, forgiving Sarah for anything she might have done to cause harm. Uh, oh. Whatever it is, Manus knows he'll be accused of it. Nobody tells you anything straight out, you're just piecing things together, and it doesn't look good for Lt. Yolland.

Doalty and Bridget appear. More English soldiers have arrived, destroying crops as they search for Yolland. This is the escalating English counter-stroke to something you haven't quite found out about. The Irish response (so far) to the English move has been indignation expressed in several languages by these seemingly unworldly people.

The playwright has Doalty tell the story with excitement and humor, and without anger. Why? To leave room for your response. If Doalty blasted you with the kind of outrage he is reporting about the others, you'd lose the role the play wants for you. Since the audience rarely duplicates an emotion found on the stage, you'd probably take on the role of discounting his story. "It can't be that bad. There must be another side." Here, the playwright is careful to leave room for your response to the English brutality, which is anger at the injustice of the violence, and a rising feeling that something must be done about it.

Owen has stopped his work on the maps. Like you, he's trying to piece things together. Who was the last to see Yolland and Maire? Was Manus involved? Bridget says, "If you want to know about Yolland, ask the Donnelly twins." Again that ominous silence when those names are mentioned. Again the feeling that these people know something you don't. Doalty changes the subject—and suddenly you realize without anyone saying another word that Yolland is dead. In life you'd be slow to arrive at this conclusion. Here in the theatre where everything is clarified and the nonessential static of the ordinary world is missing, you easily follow the clues laid down by the playwright. You're catching up to what Doalty and Bridget know, and you're ahead of what Owen knows. As I've said several times, one of the practical rules of playwriting is that someone on the stage has to know less than the audience. Put another way, even when you're struggling to catch up, your privileged place still must make you feel smarter than somebody.

The drama has escalated from the murder of horses to the disappearance of a man. Lt. Yolland, innocent and vulnerable, seemed to be at the center of the action. Like Romeo, love caused him to move from one world to another with consequences for many. Unlike Romeo, the consequence for him is death in the middle of the play.

Crucial question: Who are you going to care about now? Well, who's left? Hugh the schoolmaster is lost in drink. Maire wants to leave. Jimmy Jack is consumed by his studies. The other students are minor figures. You've been interested in Manus, but he has taken the path of running away. This shifts your focus to Owen, who comes from the Irish world, thrives in the English world, and gets along with everyone. You're beginning to watch him with an unstated question: "Whose side are you on?"

The unseen Donnelly twins are roughnecks. Owen is reasonable and responsible. Is it possible that he could go from his world to theirs? To understand a major character shift you have to find a way of marking the change as it occurs. You must have both worlds clearly in mind. You must know what world the character is in and what it will cost him to make the move to another. You must see the paths that others have taken when faced with the same choice.

This is not a novel. You can't stop and reread to get the point. Nor can you be told straight out; you won't buy it. You have to see it clearly and quickly without being told about it, which means that everything has to be set down in the most natural way so you are unaware that you are being given the coordinates and the compass for a major move—a big task for a playwright. Let's go back to the scene and see what Friel does.

Maire enters, distracted. She knows Yolland is missing and she tries hard to keep down her anxiety. She even makes a joke about Yolland trying to speak Irish to her when they parted and getting it wrong. You know she'll never see him again. You're touched by these innocent people who are slipping into something terrible and don't yet know it. Owen reassures Maire about Yolland, but his clipped dialogue lets you know he's getting nervous.

If Maire had entered weeping for Yolland or screaming about the British or the Donnelly twins, you would probably back away in embarrassment, and there would be little left for your role. You might even be tempted to fall into the role of seeing the situation as exaggerated or melodramatic and that would cripple the play.

The playwright is careful to leave frontal visceral emotions off the stage. All kinds of feelings are expressed here, but the big emotions are left for you. (In *Romeo and Juliet*, the Capulets cry out when they think Juliet is dead. You know she's not. Your knowledge is a screen that lets you put their wailing in perspective.) Maire talks distractedly about Yolland's home in England, about her geography lesson, about the haying, and then she makes a strange announcement. The new baby celebrated with comedy in act one has died. It's just another sad story for Maire; for you it's a sign that this world has no future, that these moments are the last moments of a dying way of life.

No one voices what you're thinking. Why not have one of these people say: "A way of life is dying." Then what would you think? Most likely: "Oh, come on, stop exaggerating."

Audiences instinctively try to locate a role that no one else is filling. If you're told one thing, you will tend to think another. Moments become more precious when you're the only one who notices them.

Captain Lancey enters. No more the awkward guy you could credit with correctness, if not decency. Suddenly he's nasty. All the Irish are being treated as though they are no longer humans. This is especially telling because these Irish have treated the English with great courtesy. To really feel one man's inhumanity you have to be exposed to another man's humanity. That sets a standard, and when it's violated you feel it quickly and clearly.

Owen is treated like the rest of the Irish, except he's the one who must translate the English demands: If Yolland is not found, everything will be destroyed—animals, fields, houses—and everyone will be evicted.

You are beginning to hate the English captain. You're watching Owen for his reaction. You know how he feels about the backward Irish and the forward-looking English. He works for the English. He's done well in the city. He's a realist. He's been amused by Yolland's naïve romantic vision of the country Irish. And he has seemed behind you and everyone else in grasping the situation.

Is he changing now? As he translates Lancey's orders and threats, you can feel the tension rising in him. Once he almost explodes at Lancey, then stops and continues to translate. Lancey dictates which villages will be destroyed, using the ugly English place names that Owen has provided ("Swinefort," "Burnfoot"), while Owen repeats the magical Irish names ("*Lis na Muc*," "*Bun na hAbhann*") that he has killed. Watching Owen, you feel his rising bitterness. You are beginning to want something from him. You want him to be as angry as you are.

Doalty looks out the window and mentions casually that the British camp is on fire, something that Owen has to translate for Lancey who runs out. Stroke, counter-stroke. The stakes are rising. Yolland is missing. English troopers are destroying the farms. English tents are burning. School is being abandoned. Sarah can't talk anymore. Even the sweet smell of the potato blight is in the air.

The play is rolling on its fate line. Still, everything is presented with restraint, all violence kept off stage. If this were a movie, you'd see the farms being destroyed and the English camp in flames. In the theatre, your imagination carries you. The restraint on stage allows you to feel what no one is actually voicing: Outrage. Your eyes are focused on Owen. What's he feeling? What's he going to do?

For the first time there is talk of defending themselves, calm, quiet talk. The stage direction has Doalty speaking *"almost dreamily"* as he says: "I've damned little to defend but he'll not put me out without a fight. And there'll be others who think the same as me." This is a quiet challenge to Owen. Doalty is asking him what you're asking him: "Whose side are you on?"

Owen lets the challenge slip by. He asks Doalty if they expect to defend themselves against a trained army. Doalty says: "The Donnelly twins know how." Owen sidesteps again: "If they could be found." Doalty repeats: "If they could be found." Then he adds as he leaves: "Give me a shout after you've finished with Lancey. I might know something then."

The challenge hangs in the air. Owen says nothing. You know something strong is happening inside him. You can tell by the way he picks up the Name-Book, looks at it and puts it on top of a pile of books, and then doesn't bother to pick it up when it falls to the floor. The Name-Book is Owen's work for the English. It represents the rational English-speaking-and-thinking world he has prospered in. It symbolizes the changes the new world is bringing to the backward Irish—changes that may be destroying them.

Who is thinking all this as the Name-Book falls to the floor? You are. Life doesn't often offer up symbols—small things that stand for big things. Theatre treats symbols gingerly. Anything offered directly as a symbol will be spurned by you. You'll just get annoyed with it. The playwright introduces the Name-Book as a book. It's a work product. Only slowly does it begin to stand for something larger than itself. You see that now. Does Owen see it? And more important—is he going to do anything about it? You're being carried along swiftly in the current of the play. No time to stop and reflect. And yet you have to be surefooted in your reactions. If someone is changing, you must feel it instantly.

Hugh, the schoolmaster, and Jimmy, the prize student, enter. Someone else is getting the job at the new national school. The hedge-school is doomed. Hugh is losing himself in drink and philology. Lonely drunken Jimmy announces he's getting married to the goddess Athene. Neither seems aware of the threats to their lives that are all over the countryside.

The Name-Book on the floor symbolizes the new world being imposed on Ireland. How people react to it will give you a way of quickly calculating where they stand. Hugh picks up the Name-Book and starts reading off the new English names for local Irish places. Owen grabs the book, saying it's "a mistake—my mistake—nothing to do with us." Owen's crucial moment, his test, has arrived. This is a play about language, and Owen now knows that the language in the Name-Book is wrong. You catch the importance of what he's saying so simply: his work, his life, his neutrality, his words—all wrong.

Owen is moving from one world to another. You are making a move too. You've gone from understanding what they don't understand to being the good detective on the trail the playwright has left for you. You have anticipated the future with growing hopes and fears for people you care about. Now there's something you desperately want to see.

Theatre is a study in contrasts. Characters are paired. You understand one person's action only by seeing others taking other actions. Hugh, father and master, says everyone must learn the new names. "We must learn where we live. We must learn to make them our own. We must make them our new home." Heart-breaking words from an old man who cannot stop the future.

And what does Owen say in reply? You lean forward in your seat. You demand something from Owen and you demand it now. He is the charming one, the fair-minded one, the non-political one. You demand that he feels the outrage that you feel about what's happening to his people. You demand that he say something, and you desperately want him to do something.

Quietly, Owen says, "I know where I live." At last—finally—the moment of self-knowledge. Who hears this? Who understands the meaning of it? Hugh, drunk, not able to face the present, falls back into philology. But you hear very clearly. "I know where I live," says Owen, and you hear the irony (they will all soon be evicted), and you hear the new note of determination. Owen the easy-going, Owen the go-between, has moved from one world to another. He will fight for the Irish. And at this moment only you know.

But how do you know? How can you get so much out of these simple words? If you heard them in life they would skitter past you. In the theatre, this moment has been carefully calibrated by the playwright for your instant comprehension. He's moved Owen from the world of "I've left here" to the world of "I know where I live," so that when he says these words you know what they mean, and you know what he means to do. You know what he has gained, and you know what he will lose in an unequal battle. Most likely everything, including his life.

You've taken the path the playwright has laid out for you, while all the time feeling that you have been constructing your own path. Later, as you think about it, you may retrace your steps to see how the playwright used his invisible hand to lead you from one end of the journey to the other. But, at this moment, you're not thinking, you're feeling. You feel the rightness of Owen's statement. You understand the rebellion of the spirit that will lead to rebellion in the land. You see the impact of Yolland's death and Manus' leaving and Maire's despair and Hugh's defeat and Lancey's dehumanizing. At last, you have got what you wanted.

Pause for another moment. What if Hugh had heard Owen and asked what he meant, and Owen had given him (and you) a ringing statement about Irish freedom and his willingness to die for it? That might fit another kind of play, but it's out of place in the world Friel has constructed, and it would not create the desired effect on you because it would leave you no role. If spoken directly to you (pretending to be spoken to Hugh), you'd back away, embarrassed, and the statement might even seem a bit bogus. Friel is always careful at critical moments to keep you firmly in your role, to allow you to feel what no one on the stage is expressing.

The stage cannot get you to feel something by demanding it from you. If the stage says cry, you'll want to laugh. If the stage says laugh, you won't. And if the stage says stand up and cheer, you're going to look at your watch.

When Clifford Odets wrote *Waiting for Lefty* in the thirties, he wanted the audience to join the taxi drivers in deciding to strike against the cruel bosses. He addresses the audience as though they are the taxi drivers. He even puts actors in some of the seats to get you to stand up at the end and shout: "Strike! Strike! Strike!" That kind of agitprop theatre is long gone.

Translations is not a call to action. The play is asking you to feel for Owen and Hugh and Manus and Doalty and the Donnelly twins and Maire and Yolland and Sarah, and even Captain Lancey. You, playing your distinct and separate role, are not going to cheer anybody on. You're going to watch with deep understanding.

*   *   *

You're almost at the end of the play. There's just one more thing to see, and one last adjustment in your role.

Remember again the simple but important difference between a play and a novel. You don't experience a novel in one sitting. You pick it up, put it down, skip a dull part, reread a confusing passage, and still enjoy it. You can even dislike the ending and love the novel. (Who gets through the last sixty pages of *War and Peace* with any pleasure?) A play is experienced in one sitting. And if you're not satisfied with the final image—no matter how brilliant everything has been to that point—it can turn a great evening into one that is ordinary, even disappointing. Good plays end well, and a mediocre play can be saved by a great final image.

On the Town was a 1949 musical about three young sailors in wartime on a 24-hour leave in New York (one world encounters another, all the moments precious). They're looking for adventure and romance, and they find some of each. The next morning, at daybreak, a little smarter about life and love, they disappear forever through the big gates of the Navy Yard.

Nice final image. Show over?

Not quite. After the three sailors disappear through the gates, three more sailors appear for their 24-hour leave. You don't know their names; they're just three more exuberant kids. But you know what lies ahead of them, and you are moved by their innocence (and the innocence of thousands like them). This underscores how far you've come in understanding and gives you your final role. The sailors are innocent; you are wise.

The introduction of an innocent who does not know what you know, or who has yet to learn what you have learned, or who has, for one reason or another, lost his knowledge is typical of the final moments of many plays. It's put there by the playwright to give you your final role. If everybody knew everything, there would be nothing for you to do. Like a lot of tactics in the theatre, this one is easier to talk about than to execute. It's a delicate problem for the playwright to produce an innocent without starting a new play, just as the play you've been watching is coming to an end.

'Night, Mother, a two-character play, ends with a phone call. Jessie Cates has killed herself, taking a rational way out of an unendurable life. Her mother, Thelma, is left bereft, with some understanding of the daughter she never understood in life. You have a deeper understanding, but to measure just how far you've come, there has to be someone on the stage who understands nothing, who is totally innocent. Look around, there's no one left.

Thelma picks up the phone and calls Jessie's brother and gets his wife who you've never seen nor heard: "Loretta, let me talk to Dawson, honey." How often in life have you been the innocent who gets that call? You don't yet know what's happened. No way for you to prepare yourself for the blow you're about to receive.

Here in the theatre, in your privileged seat, you are not the unprepared innocent. You've lived through the story. You have arranged your feelings. You understand what the family will have to grapple with—the self-inflicted death of a young woman. For once in your life you can experience that devastating phone call, feeling sad, but also wise.

In the final image of *Oleanna*, the professor sits quietly at his desk, the student lies on the floor. He has been stripped down from an academic who believes in thoughtful dialogue to an enraged man. She has been stripped down from confused student to feminist radical to cowering woman. He has cursed her, calling her "cunt"; she has turned away and answered to herself: "Yes, that's right."

No more illusions for either. Everything revealed in raw essence as he arranges papers and she remains on the floor.

So where's the innocent?

The professor's unseen wife, on the other end of the phone line, still has her illusions about their future. She has not been told about the catastrophe you have just witnessed. Her shock is yet to come.

She doesn't know what you know. But then—in the strange hush that falls over the play—you may begin to question what you know. Not just who was the harasser and who was the harassed, but what was the hidden unspoken relationship between the man and the woman? A lot to think about as you leave the theatre.

In the final scene of *The Elephant Man*, two men are preparing the elephant man's obituary for the newspaper. Gomm, the hospital administrator, has written a statement that is conventional, institutional, neat, and misses everything you have discovered about the elephant man—his intelligence, his touching sensibility, his imagination. Treves, the doctor who knew the elephant man and was moved by him, wants to add something, but can't pull his thoughts together with conviction.

Who knows the whole story? You do. Where are the innocents? They are the newspaper readers who will glance at the obituary and never learn anything that matters about the elephant man, unless they go to the play and sit in your privileged seat.

The final moments of Martin McDonagh's *The Beauty Queen of Leenane* feature Maureen, the crazed killer of her crazed mother, sitting alone in her house in a remote corner of Ireland. You've played your role of anticipation and have been surprised many times. You've moved back and forth in your sympathies between seeing Maureen as victim and then as oppressor. You've gone from illusion to reality. Now Maureen sits in her mother's chair, alone, listening to the radio. She's surely no innocent, and there's nobody left on the stage. The announcer's voice is heard:

> A lovely tune from the Chieftains there. This next one, now, goes out from Annette and Margo Folan to their mother Maggie, all the way out in the mountains of Leenane, a lovely

part of the world there, on the occasion of her seventy-first birthday last month now. Well, we hope you had a happy one, Maggie, and we hope there'll be a good many more of them to come on top of it. I'm sure there will. This one's for you, now.

The rest of the world, conventionally innocent, doesn't know what you have learned about life and death in those mountains. You have become wise about the secret places in people's hearts. The irony, of course, is that the ones who asked for the dedication were Mag's daughters, and the "happy one, Maggie" is now dead. All of which only you understand.

What a day Oedipus has had! He started off as the powerful and wise king of a great (though plague-ridden) city. He cursed the unknown murderer who is the cause of the plague, and then discovered that he himself is the murderer. He disdained an oracle's prophecies that he would kill his own father and marry his own mother, and then discovered that's exactly what he's done. His wife/mother hangs herself; he tears out his own eyes and prepares for exile as a homeless beggar. And everyone in the whole damn city seems to know about it.

Are there any innocents left for the final image?

Enter Oedipus's two daughters—uh, sisters—little innocent children. He embraces them (everybody else recoils from his touch). "If you were old enough to understand, there is much I'd tell you," he tells them in a large understatement, which allows you to contrast their touching ignorance with your knowledge. The daughters will eventually find out the truth, and that's probably not a scene you'd enjoy watching. Here,

they are torn from Oedipus, leaving him truly with nothing. The playwright is pitiless with Oedipus, which is why you feel such pity for him.
He is totally a creature of the will of the gods, which he has learned and
you have relearned.

There's no new character on the stage as *Hamlet* is dying in the arms of
his friend, Horatio. He says:

> Horatio, I am dead,
> Thou liv'st. Report me and my cause aright
> To the unsatisfied.

And a few moments later:

> Absent thee from felicity a while,
> And in this harsh world draw thy breath in pain
> To tell my story.

Then an innocent appears: Fortinbras, Prince of Norway, enters with his
troops. (He's not quite new, you've seen him briefly earlier in the play.)
Fortinbras looks around astonished at the dead bodies of the King,
Queen, Laertes, and Hamlet. Horatio turns to him:

> And let me speak to th' yet unknowing world
> How these things came about. So shall you hear
> Of carnal, bloody, and unnatural acts,
> Of accidental judgments, casual slaughters,
> Of deaths put on by cunning and forced cause;
> And, in the upshot, purposes mistook
> Fall'n on th'inventers' heads. All this can I
> Truly deliver.

What does all that mean? Fortinbras has no idea. But you do. Many innocents out there will be told Hamlet's story by Horatio. He doesn't have to tell you anything.

Most playwrights don't like to introduce new innocent characters at the end of the play. Rather, they see to it that there are characters on the stage who are innocent about what has occurred and don't know what you know.

Ibsen's *A Doll's House* ends with Nora leaving her husband and children. You have understood well her declaration that she has a duty to herself more important than her duty to her family. Her husband, Torvald, doesn't get it. He's still an innocent, perhaps just on the verge of understanding as the sound of the heavy door closing with finality is heard, and the curtain falls. You are the wise one, but Ibsen does give you something to think about after you leave the theatre. How long will it take for the men to catch up to the women (and you)?

Hedda Gabler ends with a gunshot. You knew she was going to kill herself. You understood her story of thwarted intelligence. She's the other side of Nora—a trapped woman who can't escape the role that middle-class Victorian life has assigned her. Hedda's treacherous friend, Judge Brack, her innocent husband, George, his innocent aunt, and the maid do not understand her as you do.

After the gunshot, which startles them, a curtain is thrown back and Hedda's lifeless body is seen. The maid and the aunt cry out, confused. The husband shrieks: "Shot herself in the temple! Can you imagine!" He knows something, but he doesn't yet understand. He's still (for one last moment) innocent. Judge Brack understands more than the others, yet even he doesn't grasp the "why" of her action. "People don't *do* such things," he says. But people do, and you know why. The momentary innocence of these characters, their confusion and partial knowledge, only emphasize how far you've come in understanding tortured trapped Hedda.

In the final moments of *Romeo and Juliet*, the bodies of the dead lovers are discovered by innocent watchmen at the tomb in the churchyard:

> We see the ground whereon these woes do lie,
> But the true ground of all these piteous woes
> We cannot without circumstance descry.

They don't understand what's happened; you do. And if you didn't know the price of causeless hatred before you sat down in your privileged seat, you know it now. The play could end here, leaving you to imagine how the Capulets and the Montagues will react when they discover their dead children. Plays like *Hedda Gabler* end before everyone sees the truth. Shakespeare doesn't do it that way. After he finishes the inner story of Romeo and Juliet with the deaths of the lovers, he still has an outer story to resolve. He's worked hard to get you to demand certain things from the stage, and he won't let you go until you are satisfied by both stories. So Shakespeare has all the innocents—Capulets and Montagues—arrive one by one to be told about the doomed children who died because of the hatred between their families. They react with horror, and then with shame and guilt. Finally, old Capulet calls Montague "brother," and Montague calls Capulet's daughter "true and faithful Juliet." Death has caused that which Romeo and Juliet desperately wanted—and what you have demanded—an end to the senseless quarrel between Montagues and Capulets, and an end to the senseless traditions that crush life.

Does everyone now know what you know? Is everyone now as wise as you? The prince has the final words:

A glooming peace this morning with it brings.
The sun for sorrow will not show his head.
Go hence, to have more talk of these sad things...

And whom will they talk to? All the innocent people in fair Verona. But, of course, they won't have to talk to you.

The final image of *Antony and Cleopatra* is a eulogy of sorts spoken over the dead bodies of Cleopatra and her attendants by Octavius Caesar, their conqueror. As a shrewd politician, he assumes Cleopatra guessed his plan to parade her before the people of Rome, and so took her own way out. He makes note of the fact (like a professional medical examiner) that none of the women are bleeding or show external swelling, and he concurs with one of his guards that it was an easy death by poisonous snakebite. Very cool, very shrewd. Then he makes his public statement:

Take up her bed,
And bear her women from the monument.
She shall be buried by her Antony.
No grave upon the earth shall clip in it
A pair so famous. High events as these
Strike those that make them, and their story is
No less in pity than his glory which
Brought them to be lamented. Our army shall
In solemn show attend this funeral,
And then to Rome. Come, Dolabella, see
High order in this great solemnity.

Question: Does Caesar speak for you? Listen:

No grave on earth shall *clip in it*

A pair so famous...

Listening to phrases like this do you say, "By golly, that guy's got a gift for finding the right words that get to the heart of the story"? If that were so, what would be your role? You would have none. You would merely be watching, and watching in the theatre without being active is death for the audience.

Luckily (or I should say shrewdly on Shakespeare's part), Octavius Caesar, with his parched, ugly phrases, does not speak for you. He's actually the least likely person to understand—or want to understand— the super-poetic passion of Antony and Cleopatra, who gave up all for love.

This is the same Caesar who entered Cleopatra's pyramid asking, "Which is the Queen of Egypt?"—probably the best single line in the play. After all you've heard and seen of Cleopatra—how she sparkles, how her beauty "beggars all description"—here's someone who can't tell the difference between the Queen and her attendants—and doesn't care.

Caesar has no feeling for beauty. He's blind to love, blind to passionate longings, blind to tragedy. He's shrewd, single-minded, says what he has to, feels nothing. That's why he wins wars and lovers lose them.

Is Caesar the innocent who appears for the final moment of the play? Innocent may not be the perfect word. He has just conquered the world. But you know things he doesn't (or doesn't care about). His lack of interest in love allows space for you to play your role of wanting— demanding—that the love of Antony and Cleopatra live and not die. Listening to him (while looking at the dead Cleopatra), you realize how far Shakespeare has brought you, the commonsensical audience, into believing in a love stronger than empire, stronger even than death.

Like *Hedda Gabler*, *The Seagull* also ends with a gunshot. After Nina, the suffering actress, runs away from Konstantin, the suffering writer, he tears up his manuscripts, then disappears into another room. Arkadina and Trigorin, the successful actress and writer, who give suffering but never seem to suffer themselves, sit down with the rest of the family to play cards.

There is a sharp sound. The people jump. You know it's a gunshot. The doctor makes an excuse. Something must have exploded in his medical case. He goes out, comes back. "Yes, that's what it was." The others go back to their game.

Then, pretending to talk about a magazine article, the doctor asks Trigorin, whose seduction of Nina started it all, to come down to the footlights where he tells him quietly that Konstantin has shot himself. In the background are all the innocents who know nothing, while you—in your privileged place—know all. Well, not all. You can only guess how each of them will react to the news.

But for these few moments, you know more than any of them. Chekhov protects your role by leaving room for you to feel, to mourn, to prepare yourself for the reactions of Arkadina, Konstantin's mother, and the others. Of course, Chekhov could have done it another way. What if Arkadina had discovered the body of her son—followed by screams, anguish, sobs? What would there be left for you to do? Nothing, except to shrink from their pain. Screams, anguish, and sobs are usually too hot for the stage. They suck the air out of your role, leaving no place for your imagination to go. Better to have calm and quiet before the collapse. Let them go back to their illusions for another few moments, while you know the truth and wait.

Where is the innocent at the end of *Uncle Vanya*? The final image is the two main characters, Sonya and Vanya, at their desks paying farm bills. A few minutes before, Vanya has told the professor he took a shot at that he will continue sending him money as usual from the estate. "Everything," he goes on, "will be just as it was."

The play appears to be ending on this everything-is-just-as-it-was note, until Vanya and Sonya speak. They started as innocents; they are innocents no longer. They understand their own lives only too well. They have both tried to find love and both failed. Vanya starts to cry. No wit or irony can cover over the fact that his life has been wasted. Sonya tries to comfort him (and herself) with words about the peace that heaven will bring after death, which you may see as one last touching illusion. They are back in their routine lives, knowing that all they can do is endure.

If you walked into the play at this moment as an innocent visitor, you would see only a scene of country life. But you are not a visitor. You have watched from your privileged seat, hoped for them, feared for them, and now, with understanding and compassion, you weep for them. So where are the innocents that allow you to play your part at the end? They are right there, just as they were at the beginning of the play. The old nurse is knitting her stocking. The mother reads her useless pamphlets. The hanger-on plays his guitar. The watchman taps outside. Everyone remains at the center of his own life and no one understands anything about anyone else. They see everything and learn nothing. Exactly as most people behave in the real world. But you are in your privileged seat in the theatre. You have seen everything and you have learned.

The final image of Chekhov's *The Cherry Orchard* is Firs, the old valet, who's been accidentally locked in the old house. "They've forgotten me," he says. How can he be an innocent? He's lived through the whole story. He should be aware that the estate has been lost, the family has left for good, the cherry orchard is being cut down, and a whole way of life is ending.

You know all this, but Firs is old and sick. "I'll sit here awhile," he says, and fusses over which coat his master is wearing, and then lies down, probably to die. His wandering mind underscores your focus. You hear the sound of the axe is it cuts into the first tree, and you—and only you—understand what it means.

What if Firs knew what was happening and could sum up the whole story and its meaning for your benefit. You'd be out of there before he finished. When your role is taken from you, you exit fast.

Sometimes the final image of a play is a return to innocence. Playwrights use different tactics to bring characters from the painful knowledge they have achieved back to innocence, and thereby keeping a space for you to play your part.

At the end of O'Neill's *Long Day's Journey into Night*, Mary Tyrone stands before her husband and her sons, totally abandoned to drugs, "*her face extraordinarily youthful and innocent*" (says O'Neill's stage direction). The drug has released her from an unendurable present and brought her back to her youthful schoolgirl illusions:

> I had a talk with Mother Elizabeth...I told her I wanted to be a nun. I explained how sure I was of my vocation, that I had prayed to the Blessed Virgin to make me sure, and to find me worthy...

You can feel for one who is too lost to feel for herself. If Mary faced reality, if she understood everything, if she wept for herself, there would be no role for you, and you would withdraw from your assigned role of pity and understanding, and might find the end of the play, featuring three men with glasses raised to their drugged loved one, melodramatic, perhaps even funny.

Othello, in Shakespeare's play, kills his innocent wife Desdemona and then—at the low point of a good man driven to an evil deed—denies knowledge of it. You are horrified. You did not want this. What do you want to see? The old noble innocent Othello. What do you get? A quick Othello rehab. He wakes up to his deed, realizes his horrible mistakes, then kills himself, but (and here Shakespeare is really at the top of his game) he does it as though he's the old noble innocent Othello killing an infidel who deserves to die. A gallant death, and you love gallant. Now you can feel pity for Othello and, sadder and wiser, mourn for him.

Blanche DuBois, in *A Streetcar Named Desire*, has suffered so much from reality that in the end she retreats to madness and becomes innocent again. She offers her arm to the young doctor who is taking her away to the asylum and speaks the famous line, "Whoever you are—I have always depended on the kindness of strangers." She does not weep for herself, allowing you to weep for her.

What about a one-person play like *Krapp's Last Tape*? The old man is not senile like Firs in *The Cherry Orchard*. He doesn't go mad. He doesn't turn back into the innocent he once was. Where's the innocent?

The final image of the play is the old Krapp listening once more to the tape of himself as a pompous young man who sees himself at thirty-nine as old and wise: "Perhaps my best years are gone. Where there was a chance for happiness. But I wouldn't want them back. Not with the fire in me now. No, I wouldn't want them back." But the young Krapp is also filled with romantic memories: "The face she had! The eyes!" The lonely old man listens to the voice of the innocent—his own voice of years ago—describing voluptuous, tactile feelings about a river, a swaying boat, a woman. He listens with grief, remorse, regret. In the old man's silent listening, you—in your seat of wisdom—realize that you will not know what he does about loss until you sit where he sits.

Betrayal begins with the sour end of an adulterous relationship. It moves backwards in time through various betrayals by husbands and wives, and returns the characters to innocence with a last scene that is the first scene chronologically, when they are all ignorant of what will happen to them. The final image is a look between two strangers. At that moment, only you can feel wise, because you're in the theatre in your privileged seat and you know what no one can ever know in real life—the future.

The old horse is dying in the final moments of *Strider*. As he dies, his mind wanders backwards in time, first to his youth when he was strong and proud, running to win the race, and then further back to his birth, his first wobbly attempts to walk, his first sight of nature, the butterfly he tried to bite...all of which allows you to weep for him because in his delirium he does not weep for himself. Dying has returned him to innocence.

Some people are innocent because they are trapped in one world and can never understand the other world until they get there. In the final image in *Our Town*, George, the grieving young husband falls in front of the grave of Emily, his young wife. She and the other dead from the town watch him calmly. "They don't understand, do they?" says the newly dead Emily. The living are innocent, only the dead truly understand life. Only the dead—and you in your privileged seat.

Some people just never learn. The final image of *Born Yesterday* is a toast given by a corrupt lawyer, who finally admits his corruption in the face of Billie Dawn's new courage and a reporter's determination to keep fighting for what's right. Here's the lawyer's toast:

> To all the dumb chumps and all the crazy broads, past present and future—who thirst for knowledge—and search for truth—who fight for justice—and civilize each other—and make it so tough for sons-of-bitches—*(to the corrupt senator)*—like you—(*to Harry Brock*)—and you—and me.

Harry stares at him, battered, and still not getting it. He's still innocent in his corruption. But you know. You desperately wanted him to be beaten and you got what you wanted. He's the only one who doesn't understand.

Are there exceptions to the rule of the introduction of an innocent in the final moments of a play? Of course. There are exceptions to everything I've written. This is art, not physics. But next time you take your privileged seat in the theatre, see for yourself if these thoughts lead you to a better understanding of what you're seeing on the stage and what your role is in the play.

Shakespeare's final image of *Macbeth* is a moment of universal celebration for the new king. The tyrant is dead. Malcolm, the legitimate heir, will be crowned. Order has been restored. Everybody's happy. We know that Shakespeare wrote the play to celebrate the crowning of James the Sixth of Scotland as James the First of England. No doubt this is why he does not present the new king as an innocent who (for example) might be unaware of new conspiracies against him. That would be good for your role, but could have caused Shakespeare to have his head cut off. Shakespeare was not only great, he was careful with kings.

Modern directors don't have to worry about decapitation (except from the critics), so they often end *Macbeth* with courtiers on the edge of the celebration with their heads together, plotting something that only you notice. I've seen one production end with the three witches creating more evil that will turn the new king into an innocent, and will make you (who knows that evil never rests) wise.

Let's look one more time at innocents in the last moments of a play—the final image of *Translations*. The inner story of love has tested the outer story of conflict between two ways of life. The result has been the disappearance and likely murder of Lt. Yolland, the English officer, followed by the eviction of the Irish farmers from their homes. Owen, a neutral Irishman, has had his moment of self-realization and has joined the rebellion against the English. He has moved from one world to another and there will be bloody consequences for many.

Owen leaves the hedge-school to see Doalty (and the Donnelly twins), a move that will seal him on the path of violence. He's giving up everything to fight in an unequal battle he is sure to lose. Manus, his brother, has taken the path of running away to another more remote part of Ireland, to try to keep the old language alive. Maire, the young Irish girl, will run in a different direction. She will leave Ireland and the Irish language, learn English and go to the new world of America. She is still an innocent, lost in the fantasy that Yolland will return. Jimmy Jack, the lonely old man, is still an innocent, lost in his drunken fantasy of marrying a Greek goddess. Hugh, the old schoolmaster, who will never get another post, knows truths about the future that are too painful to face. He sits in the doomed hedge-school, using drink to make himself into an innocent who survives by retreating into the lost, mythic Irish past.

And you? A hundred and fifty years later, godlike in your privileged seat, having completed your journey and knowing now all the tragedy that's in store for them, you watch them sadly, perhaps tearfully, and with some wisdom.

Afterword

The play is over. The audience applauds, the actors bow, go off, applause brings them back, some people get to their feet, someone yells "Bravo!" The stars bow to the audience, then to each other, and go off again.

The house lights come on. A few people get up quickly, put on their coats. Trains to catch, babysitters to pay. They sprint for the aisles, beat the crowd to the exits, and they're out of there. Others are more deliberate. They roll up their programs, put them in their pockets or purses. A handful take off their glasses and dab at their eyes with their handkerchiefs.

You join the crowd moving slowly through the clogged aisles and down the stairs. Some people are stony-faced and silent. Some are chatting. Some have that stricken look in their eyes, "I thought I knew what it would be like, but I never dreamed...." Others seem untouched, already trivializing the play, "The critics will take sticks and kill it."

One person in the back of the house does not get up, remains slumped in his/her seat, an open notebook in his/her lap. This is the author, the playwright, trying to make sense of the audience's response. Why did heads shift just there? Why the uneasy laughter over here? When did the coughing start? And why (a dagger in the heart) did those three girls glance at their watches twenty minutes before the final curtain?

The playwright is trying to figure out where he had you in your role, and where you slipped away. Soon, he or she will be joined by the director. They'll sit together in the empty theatre talking softly, while the staff picks up fallen programs and candy wrappers. What went well? What can be fixed?

Outside the theatre, the audience fragments, breaks into pieces, strangers again. The blue-haired ladies giggle as they climb aboard the bus to Harrisburg. The handful of foreigners walk off chattering in an unknown language. The two men with earrings—one older, one younger—have gone in through the stage door to greet the cast. The elderly couple discusses the acting. The middle-aged foursome is busy analyzing: "I thought it was a defense of conventional—"; "No, no, you missed the irony. It was an attack on conventional—". The three girls from Queens are trying to decide if they have time for a sandwich. The businessman stares with a vacant look on his face, waiting for his wife to come out of the ladies room.

Behind you, the theatre lobby is going dark. People are getting into cabs, headed down into the subway, walking to their cars. You're in no hurry. The aura of the play clings to your body, lingers in your mind.

Want to walk for a while?

It takes a few minutes to sort out your feelings. There's something curious here. You did your work well. You played your part. You were the good detective. You cared about the innocent and vulnerable, you divided everyone into two worlds, you chose your side, you were moved by the urgency, the threats, the hopes. You were ahead of them sometimes, behind them sometimes, always in motion, leaning forward to anticipate, jolted back with surprise.

You saw new commitments form in the inner story and test older commitments in the outer story. You saw the strokes and counter-strokes that made the stakes rise. You felt the power of the turn-around scene when illusion gives way to reality and the play changes course and finds its fate track. You experienced the deep impact of one life on another, as someone moves between worlds with consequences for many. At the end, you demanded certain things from the stage and you got them. You felt powerful, godlike in understanding, and very wise.

And now, suddenly, you realize that all you have in your head are questions. Not about the content of the play. Not about the controversial issues raised. Controversial issues in plays usually aren't very controversial to the people who actually go to the theatre. Almost always it's theatre for the already convinced, those people who rise up in knowledge and belief exactly where they sat down.

Yes, homosexuals have it bad. Yes, blacks and Latinos and children raised by Jewish mothers have it bad. Yes, it's bad in Afghanistan. It's bad in Belfast. It's bad in New York. It's bad in the suburbs. It's bad in high school. It's bad for single women. It's bad for married women. It's bad to have cancer. Doctors are bad. Lawyers are bad. Yes, there's betrayal in politics, in science, in business, and in love. And middle-aged men who cheat on their wives end up paying the price—or not. And the world is unjust—or not.

A good way to trivialize a play is to concentrate on its politics. It may make us feel good. It may stroke our convictions. But the truth is, books are much better venues for raising questions about complicated matters.

So is it a new form of theatrical presentation that haunts you now? Perhaps some new way of handling time that has dazzled you? There are, of course, always new and different methods of storytelling which can be fussed over after the show and keep bored critics occupied.

Theatre is a great teacher, but not about issues or stagecraft. The true impact of a play is different, strikes home in a different place. Many people find it hard to acknowledge their feelings after a play. That which affects them most deeply, often they don't (can't) talk about. So they discuss themes or ideas or techniques and avoid what's happened inside them, afraid to say (if they know) just how they've been moved, just how strange and off-center and even dangerous the world feels to them now.

Maybe it was your father you saw on the stage that made you weep. Maybe it was you as a child. Maybe the play tapped into your secret life with bruising insights. Or maybe you were suddenly reminded about mortality, and time became palpable. A chord is struck. Memories flood you—not about Tibet or non-linear storytelling—but about a lost lover's face, or a path not taken, or how did you get to be thirty or forty or fifty or sixty walking down a Manhattan street after a play thinking, "What have I done with my life?"

How strange. The playwright steered you into quick insights, quick judgments, and finally quick wisdom. But the good play contains a slow aftertaste of doubts, uncertainties, questions. The better the play, the more complicated the response, until you may realize that your ordinary ways of thinking aren't working anymore. Streets look different. People look different. The model of the world you carry around in your head doesn't seem to fit anymore.

Why does Oedipus run to his fate? Why do Vladimir and Estragon wait for someone who will never come? How can Neil Simon write about so much despair and make you laugh so hard? And why do the characters in Chekhov and O'Neill pursue their doomed desires so passionately? And how do they survive loss? And when Shakespeare asks over and over, "Can love defeat death?" what is your answer?

And what are your answers to the hundred other questions about art and life that buzz around you now as you stroll through the night. Yes, theatre clarifies the world by placing people in a moving architecture that gives you the consolation (if not the proof) that life has design. But by adding the clarity of design, the playwright may be falsifying life in the very act of presenting it. And yet how else can we know the world except by exploring the models that artists give us?

Faced with such imponderables and with so much unaccounted for, how can you look back on an evening in the theatre and say that it satisfied, that it gave you pleasure and delight?

Years ago I saw a play about the Kitty Genevese case. You probably don't remember the story. A young woman in Brooklyn was murdered and a couple of dozen people heard her crying out and nobody did anything to help her. A friend of mine, an excellent writer, wrote a play about it. We sat down in the theatre in Los Angeles thinking it was going to be about all those people who heard Kitty Genevese cry out and did nothing, and when it finished we all stood up and said, "Yes, that's what it was about." It was true, it was touching, it was well-written and well-performed, and it wasn't enough. It wasn't satisfying.

Some plays evaporate on the way out of the theatre. The audience laughs long and hard, they brush away a tear or two, and by the time they hit the sidewalk all they're thinking about is the dinner reservations or the long ride home.

To be truly satisfied in the theatre, you should rise up from your privileged seat at the end of the play different than when you sat down. Even if it's a classic you've seen twenty times before, you should be able to say, "I thought I knew what it would be like, but I never dreamed..."

Think of Mozart. You've heard a particular concerto a hundred times, and yet each time when that certain section ends and you anticipate the new section will begin in a certain way, in a certain key, on a certain note, with a certain ping of loudness or softness, it always starts up in a way you didn't expect (even though you've heard it a hundred times), and you take in your breath, surprised, pleased, and delighted again. That is satisfying.

A good play reaches deep. A good play reminds us about the preciousness of life. A good play gives us the hope of something that life doesn't usually provide—the possibility that understanding is out there, though we may have to knock down old ways of looking at the world and start our thinking all over again.

We don't know for certain what the Greek audience felt when they walked home from the theatre. We believe the theatre was part of their religious rites and the audience responded to a play like *Oedipus the King* with pity (smart-ass guy but still innocent) and terror (it could happen to you), which produced a collective catharsis (Aristotle's word) of those emotions, and they would return home feeling cleansed.

Shakespeare's audience did not see theatre as part of their religion, but they were a community. He used their common beliefs to make them laugh, cry, and look on with awe, and he sent them home—not cleansed—but satisfied. The modern theatre is not a religious obligation (though season ticket holders may feel that way), and the modern audience is not a community of anything. The modern playwright tends to attack rather than comfort. Ibsen attacked his audience and was banned. Shaw attacked his audience (with wit) and got rich. Athol Fugard attacked his audience and tried to bring down an apartheid government in South Africa with plays like *"Master Harold"...and the Boys* and *Sizwe Banze Is Dead.*

There are modern playwrights who try deliberately to offend, irritate, confuse, and alienate. I once had a conversation with Fernando Arrabal, the radical Spanish playwright. I asked him what he thought the role of the playwright was. He said, "I am like the captain of a ship that is sinking. My job is to give confusing orders to make the ship sink faster."

There are theatre pieces today in which concepts like "stage" and "audience" seem to be disappearing. Actors mingle with audiences, attacking them, cursing them, making love to them, occasionally treating them like members of an Italian wedding party ("You gonna dance with me?") or a Jewish bar-mitzvah ("Eat, eat!").

Is it still theatre? Are those elements still present that will put you in a privileged place, give you a unique role, and keep you and the playwright locked in a creative embrace?

Dizzy with so many post-theatre questions, you stop at a corner and take a breath. You smile at yourself. After all, it was just a play.

You remember the first play you ever saw—a road company version of *A Streetcar Named Desire* in Chicago—and feeling blown away by passions that you, at sixteen, suddenly recognized as your own.

You remember *The Peony Garden*, the sixteenth-century Chinese music drama you saw last year in New York, with the elegantly artificial girl making elegantly artificial gestures, dressed in extravagantly artificial clothes, her face an artificial mask of make-up—and the sudden revelation of the aching human heart within (which only you witnessed).

And you remember coming out of the Shakespeare Memorial Theatre in Stratford after *The Tempest*, and walking in the darkness along the River Avon, with the colored lights of the theatre reflecting in the water and the swans glistening white in the shallows, where for a moment you stopped to think of the words of the old sorcerer:

> Be cheerful, sir.
> Our revels now are ended. These our actors,
> As I foretold you, were all spirits, and
> Are melted into air, into thin air;
> And like the baseless fabric of this vision,
> The cloud-capped towers, the gorgeous palaces,
> The solemn temples, the great globe itself,
> Yea, all which it inherit, shall dissolve;
> And, like this insubstantial pageant faded,
> Leave not a rack behind. We are such stuff
> As dreams are made on, and our little life
> Is rounded with a sleep.

And then, satisfied, sometimes richly so, you take the arm of the one you came with—husband, wife, lover, friend—and start for home.

Index